LIVE FOREVER

LIVE FOREVER
DREAM BIG, BIG DREAMS
THAT ONLY A CHILD
COULD DREAM

Russ Meyers

PUBLISHED BY

BIGBIGDREAMPUBLISHING.COM

First published in the United Kingdom 2010

ISBN 978-0-9561373-1-9

Copyright © Russ Meyers 2010

All rights reserved. No part of this publication may be reproduced, stored in or introduced into a retrieval system, or transmitted, in any form, or by any means (electronic, mechanical, photocopying recording or otherwise) without the prior permission of the publisher.

This book is sold subject to the condition that it shall not, by way of trade or otherwise, be lent, resold or hired out,

DEDICATION

When you've got big, big dreams - keep your eye on the prize. Dreamers of the day, as T. E. Lawrence would describe you, you know who you are and how you must seize with both hands right now the opportunity to leverage uncertainty into opportunity and fulfill your destiny as it unfolds before your eyes, because your time is most definitely now. You need to know and be re-assured that you are in exactly the right place at precisely the right time to act on an intuitive and growing belief in yourself and your destiny.

The fact that you are taking the time to read this book means without doubt you are attracted to the big, big dreams within you, and that you **can** be everything you want to be...and so much more. The first step is to decide. Then move. Everything else has already arrived.

CONTENTS

FOREWORD ix
INTRODUCTION xi
WARNING!! xix
ABOUT THE AUTHOR... xxi
WHAT YOU WILL GAIN FROM THIS BOOK xxiii
INTO AND OUT OF A RECESSION...MAYBE 1
BREAKING BAD NEWS 5
A Pure Adrenalin Rush... 15
Don't just dream it – Do it now..................................... 35
Winners... 39
The Ultimate DNA... 39
Become Irresistible...
because there's just so little competition 47
Giant Characteristics... of Big, Big Dreamers 49
Tips for the top 51
BELIEFS...The leverage to Success 53
More on the unreasonable nature of a Big, Big Dreamer.....57
Think Opposites...Think Why not? 63
Ask with Audacity and with Skill... 65
NO TURNING BACK... 71
Find your passion and you will find your purpose................73

Talk yourself up... (If you don't no-one else will)...................75

On Feeling Awesome..77

**Challenge fear –
by asking quality questions
 and expecting positive answers**... 81

Plan to Succeed..83

Time: The Most Valuable Commodity....................................85

**Run With Your Big, Big Dreams
as if your Life depended on it**...89

Resources and Acknowledgements...93

FOREWORD

Barack Obama and embracing big, big dreams

Let's take a trip back in time. Go back to late 2008 and, like most people, maybe you were attracted to the TV or the Net to witness the tenacious, charismatic and electrifying journey of a relatively unknown black Illinois Senator called Barack Obama attempting to become President of the Mightiest power in the world, the United States of America. Facing up to the not inconsiderable power and influence of the Clinton dynasty, Obama had squared up to and won a seemingly 'unwinnable' seventeen month-long primary campaign with Hilary, followed up by an apparently 'unloseable' five month Presidential campaign against John McCain.

The inauguration of Barack Obama as the 44th President of the United States took place on Tuesday, January 20, 2009. Watching this man's inexorable drive toward the White House we looked on, fascinated as this unknown challenged and changed both convention, conviction and history, raising record amounts of funds and speaking to great gatherings of people. For the first time a Presidential Candidate was using the social network sites Facebook and Twitter, with supporters everywhere calling for support throughout the nation to embrace change, to throw out negativity and cynicism and unite to reach out for a new and better way of life via the audacity of hope. You know, perhaps we can agree that these times are hard, but what if the world has struck lucky and stumbled across a leader of the Western World most people only dreamed of, but felt too powerless to effectively exert any influence. I found myself saying out loud what if we have a man of hope and big dreams, who mixes hard work with both in order to succeed... a man who implores everyone to do the same, including a Ten year old boy asking for advice on how to succeed. The then Senator Obama left the Ten year old (and all of us) with a stunning call to action that the young man will remember for the rest of his life...which was to 'dream big dreams and imagine yourself doing the greatest thing in the world'. Without doubt it is this same call to dream big, big dreams, to follow them come what may...to face up to what has been, and for many still is, a bitter wind of recession and to go within yourself and without in order find your true strength, beauty and purpose and go on to achieve your biggest of dreams.

INTRODUCTION

Welcome to a very, very special tribe, the coming together of a new generation of big, big dreamers who want more, more than just possessions and material reward, more than respect and admiration...welcome to a world of people who want to leave something great, a legacy, want to build something with their big, big dreams that will have great value and benefit beyond their lifetime. People maybe just like you with child like dreams energised with the ferocious hunger of a fully grown lion and the evolutionary hunter's instinct that clearly states to all concerned that come what may, you will not be denied. Big, big dreamer have you wondered how in this very moment you are finding yourself being drawn to probably the most exciting and most disturbing of times in history in order that you may achieve you're most treasured of dreams? Yes you read that right; I said THE MOST EXCITING and paradoxically, the most DISTURBING OF TIMES in history! Because despite the worst recession in possibly 80 years and the ensuing financial turmoil throughout the world, we as the unique species on this earth are on the verge of the most gigantic breakthroughs in health, business, education and economics ever witnessed. Yet what is even more spine tingling and hair raising is that we don't quite know what's coming next, even when it's right in front of us, never mind that which is about to hit us from leftfield…visa via another 'black swan'. We face unprecedented growth levels in world population and the associated food, shelter, energy and Geo-Political issues that naturally trail in its wake. The sheer speed and uncertainty of change and consequential chaos leaves us breathless, unsettled and in awe, yet still it never dawns upon us, each of us to stop, to stop running away from our fears or toward someone or something outside of ourselves that we believe will be the game changer in our lives and give us the security and good feelings we crave. So look, before you come off the next curve and the next big thing in your life, STOP RIGHT NOW. Stop and just breathe into your biggest and wildest of child-like dreams, into the stuff of life, love, purpose and energy that lights up an inferno within you. Try it right now, let go of everything and just breathe, exalt in appreciation for all you are, all you have been and all that is yet to come. Whether you're broke, a steady Eddie or in the land of abundance, trust me on this one, that's right just do it…AND BREATHE. That said, and only when you're absolutely ready, let's go do what Walt Disney, Da Vinci, Steve Jobs and all the big, big dreamers did and will always do… lets go play, get excited, get hungry, passionate, and creative, lets trust, thrust forward and make a decision to never ever quit on making our biggest dreams come true…LETS GO BUILD SOMETHING THAT WILL LIVE FOREVER.

You know, just as you are now breathing life into your dreams I wonder if you are already noticing that simultaneously we have the most awesome tipping point events occurring in our society that are changing how we think and perceive life itself, events that are precipitating huge, no turning back paradigm shifts about what is and isn't possible for the human race, such as Usain Bolt's breathtaking 9.58 second 100 metres record set in Berlin in August 2009. The transplant of a human windpipe grown from stem cells, a surgical breakthrough of almost limitless potential in the years to come. Bloom Energy, a Silicon

Valley company have created a potential ecological breakthrough with an unbelievably small power plant-in-a-box that installs in minutes. The company's aim is for you to generate your own electricity with the box and the great thing is its all wireless. The bigger picture for the company is to eventually replace the big power plants with these small boxes the way cars replaced the ubiquitous horse power.

New and seismic shifts are taking place across the globe as I write, the like of which have never been seen before. The old certainties, which where even not so long ago the new certainties, are coming under increasing strain. Microsoft is threatened by Google which in turn looks over its shoulder at Facebook and Twitter which in turn looks back at Foursquare, a location based social networking site, and at every new start-up wondering if it's the next big thing. The internet is offering opportunities to people across the world, many whom had never dared to dream that change would come so quickly and so near to home. Well it has and there is more, much more to come, and if like me, you are a sensor of change, an intuitive big, big dreamer and doer always looking for the second bounce of the ball you will already know why you have read thus far.

Yes, you are already acknowledging your big, big dreams, and yet you're not a sucker to the realities you see happening in Iraq, Gaza, Afghanistan, Iran, Pakistan, Burma. North Korea and many other areas of change and conflict, indeed they are deeply troubling...maybe you're even seeing, hearing and experiencing this every day on a deeply personal level and your big, big dream is to create change that will live forever in one of these regions...yet simultaneously, you out and out refuse to be blown away by economic downturn, upturns and the sensationalistic, drama queen gloomeisters on the street, TV, newspapers, radio and the net. You may describe yourself as both liberator and liberated. You are not fooled, blindfolded, dragged, gagged or led by what you see and hear and you are smart enough to be aware of when, where, what, why and how you're being sold every day on someone else's plan for you. You see through Agendas...

political, economic, social, cultural, emotional, and the ultimate sale of fear and/or greed so you go by what you intuit, what you feel in your gut and sense to be true. You are ready to go for your big, big dream! Scared? Maybe! Energised? Most definitely, because deep inside you know there has never been a better time to go, never been in history a successful big, big dreamer who isn't or hasn't been scared in some form or other, before finding a way to leverage and redefine that same fear to their advantage. You are the natural inheritor of Soldier and Adventurer T.E. Lawrence's description of the dreamer of the day, of whom he described within his autobiographical book *the seven pillars of wisdom*[1]. Your rise, due in no small part to a cataclysmic series of financial and economic blunders, greed and abuse on a scale and speed the world has, in all probability, never witnessed before, coincided with the incredible rise to power and leadership of Barack Obama, President of the United States of America. Now I don't claim to know everything about Obama, nor do I go door to door proselytising that he's all things to all men and women, many have their doubts for instance about how he has handled the BP Oil leak and Afghanistan, but what I do know is all that I see and sense, and what I sense is a guy who is out there walking his talk, taking on vested interests in Healthcare, Wall Street and the Auto industry and winning. A guy who is following his big, big dreams, helping people like you and me believe that anything is possible, that it really is worth dreaming big, big dreams and building something positive, something that will last and live forever.

Of course cynics will deride him, quite probably all the way through his term, that's what often happens to big, big dreamers. Like you, he is right now and will do so in the future, face up to titanic battles to get the right things done, witness the Health Care Bill and the challenges he has come up against before getting it through the House and signed into law. Yet, and if we needed more evidence of the power of Big, Big Dreamers to move people to take action and change the world, take a look at his approval ratings around the globe, especially with the young;

don't you too get a sense that we may be in the midst of the best opportunity for big, big dreamers like you and me to achieve our greatest dreams! So let me ask you a question, in the face of these amazing events and people just like you making incredible moves into what really juices them...tell me, what prevents you, no I mean really prevents you from going out right now and becoming the remarkable person you truly are, I mean what could it have been that used to get in the way of you changing your inner and outer world?...that's right nothing, nothing but excuses, false fears and someone else's rules for your life. Its true isn't it? So go now and run for your life with your dreams and make them happen, and if you need more leverage on moving into action think on this. If you were in Haiti, or Afghanistan or any number of countries around the world where opportunities to achieve big, big dreams are often so limiting and disempowering, how far do you think any of these people would go for your freedoms, your opportunities, what would they give to see and experience the opportunity to add value to peoples' lives, cultures and environments as you have right now. And let me twist your arm just a little bit further (If I have to), imagine what you may be like in five, ten and twenty years time, when you're frozen in regret, time and the bitter, bitter cold of guilt and remorse because you did nothing except to buy into the fear and drama of it all, and you stayed put or maybe tried a little, moved a little, did a little to assuage the guilt, but ultimately achieved nothing with your life. Simultaneously, tell me, or better still answer this question for yourself, what does it feel like as you realize at this very moment that if this call to action is perceivably too much for you, too big for someone like you...how does it feel to know that you haven't got to do this stuff...that nobody is putting a gun to your head and saying *Go* now, just because you can! You can if you want just let all the good stuff go, let it die.

Yet wait up...imagine this, what would it be like to create, to devise and build things and services that people want from you, that they might like or maybe even love, something incredible, original and great that absorbs you and that's not just based on what money you can make or how many you can sell. (Apparently this is what the Geeks at Google do... asking questions like 'is this cool'? Or 'will people want this'?).

It's a truism is it not that those dreaming big, big dreams may be young or old, of any nationality, gender or in any kind of relationship. People can be broke, breaking or broken, maybe moving in or out of care, unemployment, and redundancy or even prison. A big, big dreamer may be a single mum, alla J K Rowling who in 1997, as you may know was a single mum, living in a rented flat, surviving on part-time earnings and benefits and just eleven months later securing a hugely lucrative publishing deal, because when you're holding big dreams neither your colour, money status or your health matters, dreaming big dreams is an unalienable right, a freedom to all. What really matters and I believe to be certain in this world of beauty, brilliance and miracles is that we have another universe, a parallel universe if you will, a universe of volatility, violence and evil that left to its own devices would subvert, subsume, distort and destroy all in its path, and so we operate out of and within an environment of conflicting energies and chaos oft accompanied by unnerving fears, demands and uncertainties. Tell me, in your opinion which universe benefits from your inertia, from the void of not having your talents, gifts, energy and drive? Which of the Universes' leaves you with a call to action asking, no demanding of you, perhaps more than ever before, a willingness to embrace and honour your biggest dreams in different ways and at different levels from anything you may have attempted before. Which world badly needs you to be all you can be and more, and which world offers you more joy, flow, love and learning than you can imagine...my calculated guess is that you've always known the answer to that one, haven't you.

So, let no one be in any doubt there are big changes ahead, no matter where you are in the world, and believe me you want to be a part of it, not apart from it, because this is it, everything you've ever experienced, including your celebrations and your biggest failures have all conspired to lead you to this point in your life.

So put your crash and burn dilemmas and indecision behind you, because this is your final wake up call. Come on, breathe, that's it, that's right, take a couple of deep breaths and feel the energy of having your fabulous inner power ignited and within reach because it's time to say YES...YES to life, to fear, failure and doubt, they come with the territory, so go and go now toward fulfilling your purpose, your mission, because this time, this book and this momentous period in your life is your delicious and urgent call if you will, to imagination, to big, big dreams, to action and a life that will live forever. You need to know all is well, your dreams are alive, and your timing is impeccable. Preparation and opportunity are romancing again. Now go, lead from the front, draw good people toward you as you learn from the past, appreciate the present and leave the falsity and lies of fear behind you as you look toward the magnificent, bright sunlight of your future leading, drawing and enrapturing everything and everyone you touch.

WARNING!!

I cannot ask you to buy into your big dreams without issuing a warning to those of you who are maybe faint of heart, perhaps thinking of retreating, becoming passive watchers and listeners by day, because sooner than one might think, a person can find him or herself disenfranchised, derailed and discouraged by those who become rich via the sale of fear, scarcity and poverty thinking. So you must be aware that like a thief in the night some people are apt to steal your big dreams from you, slowly but surely turning you into a vanity dreamer of the night. You can also be sure, very sure, that losing both time and momentum will cost you dearly because these twin forces will not wait forever for you because they will pass you by in the twinkling of an eye, as surely as night follows day.

ABOUT THE AUTHOR

As owner and creator of DreamBigBigDreams.com and BigBigDreamPublishing.com, Russ has spent the last fifteen years of his life focusing on how he can help people young and old, male and female, the healthy and those physically and emotionally challenged achieve their big, big dreams. He has worked with both Rich and poor and many in between in order to reach deep within to the life giving energy that takes people from both emotional and financial darkness and bankruptcy to big dreamer wealth on multiple levels. Having come from a working class background, leaving school with no formal qualifications and an unhealthy disillusionment with what was he perceived to be on offer, Russ found himself with a not-so-wealthy image of himself and facing up to a dream in fast flow meltdown. Working within poorly paid, uncertain and extremely challenging environments, Russ was encountering a black hole, a void if you will that threatened his very existence and a life so much less than that which he dreamed of as young boy. And so it transpired that the early, wonderfully Camelot-like one thousand days of schoolboy energy, high hopes and even bigger dreams of becoming the greatest footballer the world had ever seen, was fast becoming dark, obsessive, anaemic and destructive.

It was at this point Russ began what he only later would discover was a trial by fire, a battle for his very survival, and only after many of his own very personal and traumatic failures, did he begin to discover from luck, experience and discussions with very successful and seemingly unstoppable big, big dreamers that in order to achieve big, big dreams, often against a backdrop of seeming emotional darkness, failure and despair, you must, you absolutely must dig deep inside to find what you never knew existed...what Russ calls an unreasonable and irrational never quit belief in yourself, an attitude to failure and success that sets you apart from everyone you know. (The reason why it's an unreasonable belief is that so few people are prepared to follow beyond what they define as reasonable...as rational, as enough, despite what they say) Because learning to come back again and again you are continually taking unreasonable perspectives and actions thereby increasing your courage and confidence. So by acting on what you are learning and meant to do with your life...that's it! You learn, and then go again, continually moving, extending your limits and developing something that Donald Trump calls **Momentum.**

WHAT YOU WILL GAIN FROM THIS BOOK

One of the many changes you may notice as you find yourself working and enjoying the unreasonable, courageous and confidence building attitudes of this book into your life will be the deletion and obliteration of poor beliefs and nullifying fears that used to keep you from starting your big, big dreams and that once left you with a feeling of being caught like the Titanic fast approaching an unavoidable and gigantic iceberg. Simultaneously, as you read on and begin taking actions toward your big dreams you will have installed, imprinted and re-imprinted more useful beliefs, perspectives and behaviours into your nervous system that work for you every day, helping you to turn, again and again, seemingly bad situations into seriously advantageous ones. You will in fact have gained everything you need to begin, sustain and drive you toward your big, big dream. Now that's a thirst quenching and tasty thought is it not, because as you learn from increasingly evident role models of success around you and by focusing on what you do best, you can, in uncommon moments, begin to notice an acceleration in your learning, confidence, and results that come from your daily, focused and consistent actions. Because that's what successful people like you do, every single day, they are relentless and remorseless. Like you, successful people have come to recognise that they are powerful, cybernetic-goal orientated machines, marching toward the achievement of their big dreams. Have you not realised yet that we all love to dream, set goals and hit them? Why? Because we totally love it! We are hard-wired to learn and succeed from birth. We inherently know how to survive and thrive. We just forget to remember because life is often so much easier today in our culture and civilisation than when our forefathers had to literally survive by their wits and rely on the fight or flight chemical and nervous system responses of our bodies. Yet it's also a reality of our culture that we haven't the luxury of choosing not to learn or to stay the same. If we quit and do nothing, then we starve, move backwards and die. For example, thousands of years ago if we moved from the relative safety of the cave into uncharted territories because we needed food, and were attacked by a *Tyrannosaurus Rex,* then we would have needed to move quickly, very quickly and regroup, take stock and find another way to our objective, and if that failed find another way...why? Because if we didn't we would have starved and eventually died. Now substitute starving for failing to develop a big vision, a big dream. In my opinion, and I understand that this can sound harsh but if we deny or reject our gifts, then we die, somehow in someway...both metaphorically and literally.

Seriously, maybe you haven't thought about it yet that there is a natural correlation between hunger for food and hunger for hope, and you may come to know and address this sooner rather than later...my passion is that you do it right now. You know I could tell you to start now without delay because timing is crucial, and that when you start you will have picked up your own speed and momentum quite naturally, I may even have decided not to shout through these pages, but to whisper to your unconscious to listen closely to how you will feel happier and more determined than you have felt in your whole life as you uncover the magic inside the first few pages of this book and more importantly, inside yourself. Perhaps you're already discovering the ingredients of the potion while I appeal to the bigger picture within your imagination, but then again I may do that only as fast as you allow yourself to spread the outrageous feelings and energy that drive you to discover just what is possible right now in the moment as you move effortlessly toward the magnetic and magical source of your big, big dreams. But of course I may not do any of these things because all of this is for you and so much more are for you to pleasurably discover, uncover and learn from, after all many people want things to be simple, but not too simple, do they not? Yet of course what I do know is that by some very simple hypnotic logic and suggestions a person, maybe even just like you, could quite easily find yourself in wonderfully uncharted territories almost too beautiful to the naked eye as you make and take decisions that propel you to a wonderful and majestic point of no return. But again, it is for you to decide when and now to develop a new and improved skill set either through trial and error or the faster method of learning via modelling someone who has already done what you want to do. You know, a friend once said to me, 'Russ, life all comes down to just a few moments in time', and I acted on that perception. Now I ask you that same question, with this addendum, *'what if this was one of those moments in your life, I mean now you come to think about it, one of those moments that suddenly stopped you in your tracks and you just knew life would never be the same again. What a thought, quite staggering isn't it that a person can do that anytime soon they choose.* What are you doing, tomorrow, next week, next month that is leading you toward the most incredible years of your life?

Finally, you may also discover as you move through the pages of this book and indeed the pages of your life, that at both a conscious and unconscious level, crucial differences between why people once passed you by and why others want to be around you are revealed, which means when you truly watch and listen to what and how people say things to you, a person can find out precisely what others value about you and why. They will tell you what they are moving away from, and conversely what they want most from you, and how you might give them what they want. You will learn that by adding value and providing solutions to something that causes people pain, both real and not so real, you can reach that break-through moment in your personal life that tells you all things are possible to the healers of the world.

Further, and by far and away one of the best things you will discover is that the real beauty of it all, as Einstein so wonderfully put it, is that either everything is a miracle or none of it is, and de facto the best way to achieve your big dreams as all big, big dreamers eventually experience is that far from seeking fame, fortune and glory per se, when you're bigger purpose is to help others achieve their very own big dreams, indeed miracles, you cannot not connect with the wonder of it all as the reality becomes for you and those you inspire... a life of appreciation, abundance and value that will live forever.

A CAVEAT

Yet before you put your work overalls on and go out and make your BIG, BIG Dreams even more of a reality, you need to know that there is one caveat to everything this book offers you and it is this. I will not BS you with regard to money. I cannot and will not guarantee you will become a multi-millionaire or even a millionaire along the way upon achievement of your big dreams, if that is indeed what you want, I can't do that. This is because money is often the by product of you're doing something very, very well. Some call the making of money just a way of keeping score, a score that's intrinsically related to how well you provide value and benefits toward healing the pain or orchestrating a series of pleasures upon a group (or tribe) of people that you have found, who both want and need what you have to offer, and of course are willing and able to pay for it.

*"I don't dream at night, I dream all day.
I dream for a living"*

Steven Spielberg

"If you think you're too small to have an impact, try going to bed with a mosquito"

Anita Roddick

Simultaneously, in today's post-recession market place and just when we needed some ray of sunshine and hope, people are noticing the rise of an historical and recurrent phenomenon. It has its roots in every downturn or recession you care to examine, from 1929 and the great depression, to 1973 and the Oil crisis, then through to the late 70's and early 1980's Iranian revolution and yet another energy crisis, to the 1990's manufacturing and sales decline, before closing out with the great Dot.com collapse of 2000 and the 2008/2009 financial crisis which swept across the globe resulting in the worst recession in nigh on 80 years. This phenomena consists of groups of people around the world who are changing their perception and colouring of a recession from a lizard brain fear of danger, adversity and survival, to a consuming belief that a recession is a time for an alchemical mix of left and right brain logic and creativity, which in turn produces an opening for those two great allies, preparation and opportunity to once again arise for those who are perceptive and courageous, looking one step ahead at the new realities that are appearing everywhere.

At this point it's important to remind you that at one time during the 70's and 80's during a downturn, Bill Gates (Microsoft) was a big, big dreamer, so to Steve Jobs (Apple). In 1972 Richard Branson opened a chain of Virgin record stores just before a massive U.K. energy crisis crippled the country and led to blackouts and a three day working week. Once again, another big, big dreamer seeing and doing things against the accepted norms, at a time of perceived 'crisis'.

And Of course who can forget the late, great and much missed Dame Anita Roddick, she too also at one time was a big, big dreamer, having to succeed, in order to survive day-to-day with her children. Ditto, Oprah, Madonna and many, many others... Incredible stories every-one meant for you to learn from and put to use, whilst staying true to yourself.

I have coined the term *Fresherneur*[2] to describe all new big, big dreamers. The term Fresherneur is an amalgam of the word Fresher, (first year student) and entrepreneur. I have found a fascinating definition of a student, being from the Latin second type conjugation verb 'studere', meaning to 'direct one's zeal at'. Hence an entrepreneurial student is one who directs zeal at a subject (Source: Wikipedia). And isn't that a brilliant, living, breathing description of a big, big dreamer? To direct one's zeal and energies at whatever you are focusing on. An Entrepreneur is (as if you needed me to tell you) one who applies innovation within the context of business to satisfy unfulfilled market demand. (Source: Joseph Schumpeter 1934) So, go ahead and direct your zeal at what you want to have happen in your life, study it with a passion, love it and own it now.

And so we see that the Fresherneur is by nature a big, big dreamer, curious as to the significance of the times, about what is missing, overlooked in the fog and fear of a downturn, and which can now be lit up and leveraged during the first sunlit rays of a recovery. Fresherneurs are people who love to learn, to act boldly with courage and faith. Perceptive, they are open to new information, opportunity and risk, taking actions that others will not. Make no mistake Fresherneurs pay great respect to their big, big dreams, to cultural and social change and to lack...whether perceived as good or bad. They believe that the desire to dream and dream big, to achieve dreams with purpose and value would not be so bold, would not be seared in their hearts and minds if it were not written within their neurology. They believe that somehow, someway they will eventually make their big dreams a reality.

Big dreamers draw inspiration from multiple sources and one in particular, that of T E Lawrence's depiction of the Dreamers of the day from the book 'The Seven Pillars of Wisdom', within which Lawrence describes the beauty and dangers that lay ahead for dreamers of the day. Lawrence goes on to contrast the dreamers of the day with the paucity of life given to dreamers of the night, who upon waking find that all has been vanity, all to no avail. He continues to describe dreamers of the day as people taking daily actions using brain and muscle; sweat and constant thinking to make others see their vision, to make their dreams come alive...make them come true.

A striking paradox, post-recession, is that Fresherneurs AKA dreamers of the day may still be in situ, i.e. in a job or perhaps in a job under threat, or on reduced working hours. People just like you who may be finding themselves in a career with a future unknown or one wracked with perpetual boredom and uncertainty, or perhaps you're unemployed, as millions across this ever shrinking planet come to terms with the global nature of this recession and it's after effects. In the U.S. alone over seven million jobs have been lost since the start of the recession late 2007 sending unemployment rates to 10%, or over 15 million people unemployed, the largest number since 1983. Within Europe, as I write the U.K fares no better with 7.9% rates of unemployment equivalent to nearly 2.5 million out of work. Spain finds itself in an even worse position with 17.9% unemployed or just over 4 million people without a job.

Yet herein lay the potential golden egg because emerging alongside this 'crisis', and despite the global cause and effect fallout, big, big dreamers are in a prime position to go now and put to use technological change and simplifications that have made the marketing and selling of information, values, goods and services to people across the globe, easier and cheaper than ever before.

As Fresherneurs are not always owners of capital or employees of labour they can and will create, innovate and execute plans quickly and ruthlessly from within any environment and context using whatever resources are available. As an example even though I have relatively low level technological skills I found a way to design, market and sell EBooks across the globe inside thirty minutes using an array of simplified applications on the internet. No situation is a barrier to the Fresherneur. The common denominator for all Fresherneurs is that they believe in the beauty and integrity of their big, big dreams, yet they know that beauty alone will never be enough...they also take relentless action every day toward their achievement. They do something that moves them closer and closer. They know their current situation is not their final destination. Instinctively big, big dreamers like you know that your time and your highest purpose cannot and must not be denied, lest you waste precious time, talent and opportunity.

You know. born winner, even though you have your doubts and fears like all of us, I say to you, you can conquer them, face them down and become everything you dream of. The contents of this book has been designed to help you make your important moves quickly and with sureness of step, to come face to face with what every Fresherneur, big, big dreamer has always come up against and had to overcome, namely fear. Fear of failure, fear of embarrassment, of rejection, of loss, loss of friends who don't want (or can't) make the journey with you, loss of family, relationships and the seemingly sweet, sweet, just too hard to give up... comfortable life.

It is with this in mind that I ask you a very important breakthrough question and it is this. It concerns an idea running through the very spine of this book, and this idea is contained within a belief, a belief in your own personal power to succeed. Beliefs, naturally positive beliefs, are fundamental to your success, yet we know they are just a collection of thoughts, feelings and emotions, basically ideas or perceptions built around something, often giving us a sense of certainty that can be so profound that they influence your most important moments, moments which swing decisions and powerfully influence what something means to you, such as events, criticism, praise, decisions and direction, and what kind of actions you may or may not take in response.

Not an ephemeral, esoteric kind of self belief, which would be wonderful if it just magically materialised, but the kind of self belief that starts small, organic in nature, growing daily according to your actions, dependent on you for water, sun, soil and growth. In fact this strong self-belief is a foundational theme, the platform for every movement forward we make, a self belief that is as defining as it is transformational, underpinning everything we have talked of within this book and its value to you.

The breakthrough question is – if you were offered a once in a lifetime chance to be remarkable, to live an unreasonable, purpose driven stand out from the crowd, rich, confident, value enhancing life... would you take it? Can you imagine what it would feel like being advised by someone you love and respect, someone you perhaps once dreamed of being close to, talking you through the adoption of a powerful life changing belief, a time proven belief of a proven winner, the type of winner who never accepted no as final or personal, a winner with a pulsating, delicious imagination and tenacity to move forward toward becoming what you were always meant to be and one who goes on to make their big dreams a reality with relatively zero finances and resources...could you ever imagine this scenario for yourself?

Can you imagine seeing through the eyes of a Richard Branson, an Oprah Winfrey, an Obama, a Steve Jobs or better still a Churchill as they look upon you with an encouraging gaze. Can you stretch yourself to see what they see, feel what they feel, and hear what they hear and say as they faced their biggest challenges. Because that's precisely what's on offer, Could you take on this one belief to make your biggest dreams come alive and achievable or do you believe like so many others that success has to be more complex? Has to be for someone else! Are you like millions of other fantasy dreamers cornered and brought to a standstill like a frozen rabbit in the glare of car headlight? Will you still find a way to deny yourself? Still find a way to tie yourself up in knots listening to the dream stealers, the sometimes friends, and peers that would deny you and keep you in a phony comfort zone which in reality is a worse fate than any you may encounter going for your big dreams. Because, when you've listened to the doubters, and long given up on your big dreams you may find yourself looking back at the glory moments in time and wishing,' I should've done that, I could have done that and if only I'd done that... only to find you have lost momentum and your time has simply passed you by. Belief is so crucial to your survival and thriving. I have heard many people offer advice on attitude, confidence, and goal setting and not a few times offer a Machiavellian like set of beliefs, such as 'you need to run a tight ship, stomp on everyone else or be stomped on', or how about 'you need to bust your xxxxs every day in order to succeed', or even that 'you need to screw people or be screwed, because it's a bad dog eat dog world out there'. For all this 'advice', In my experience I have lived with one central and core belief that every hugely successful big, big dreamer would repeat to you straight off the bat, eyes closed and it is this... that you must consume, digest and practice every day the momentous, motivational and inspirational blueprint of intent that Winston Churchill spelled out to the pupils of a Harrow School in England on October 29th 1941, Just six months after the terrible bombing of London during the Second World War. Yes, the very same Churchill recently voted the greatest Briton to have ever lived, who on that day spoke to and implored his young audience to... **'Never give in, never give in, never, never, never – in nothing, great or small, large or petty –never give in except to convictions of honour and good sense'**. Someone I respect very much said to me some time ago, **why don't you just try this belief out in your life** and then notice how well it fits before saying yes and adopting it. So I did and I've lived this belief for all it's worth, through every difficulty, failure, fear and rejection I've ever come across and I've never let myself down yet.

INTO AND OUT OF A RECESSION...MAYBE

One of the first things you may become aware of as this one belief of 'never ever giving in', of not quitting starts to permeate your life, is the fact that you are becoming the living embodiment of a new and confident way of living. A confident and limiting belief busting way of discovery and exploration that leads to a freeing, renewing and re-energising big, big dreamer Spirit inside of you that powerfully transforms your vision and dreams into working plans and actions moving you toward the step by step achievement of your big dreams.

Yet whether this financial and economic crisis hit you yesterday, today or perhaps over the coming weeks and months, in the form of heightened fears for the future, anxieties over public service cuts and pressures from mortgage payments, perhaps reduced access to credit, late payment fees, higher charges or even threatened job security and unemployment, there is no doubt that we have been (and perhaps still are) in the perceptual eye of a recession the like of which will continue to ask questions and raise opportunities for you over the next months or years, opportunities that you must seize upon like a hawk watching its prey, manoeuvring and watching for the moment to strike and when that time arrives, striking ruthlessly, relentlessly and remorselessly.

DREAMERS OF THE DAY

"This, therefore, is a faded dream of the time when I went down into the dust and noise of the Eastern market-place and with my brain and muscles, with sweat and constant thinking, made others see my visions coming true. Those who dream by night in the dusty recesses of their minds wake in the day to find that all was vanity; but the dreamers of the day are dangerous men and women, for they may act their dream with open eyes, and make it possible"
T.E. Lawrence – Dreamers of the day... The Seven Pillars of Wisdom

BREAKING BAD NEWS

BREAKING NEWS... what exactly do the media mean when sending this almost incessantly hypnotic like message of breaking news? For what purpose this breaking news? What and who classifies the news as breaking news? Is breaking news, I wonder, some hitherto unimaginable and previously thought impossible breakthrough that will revolutionise our world with breathtaking possibilitics and implications? Is it an event so vitally important that we need to know because it affects what we do at that particular moment in time? No. My inspired guess is that the meaning of the breaking news is nothing more than to deliver a daily diet of bad, fear invoking, demotivating and delineating information that separates us from the moment and each other, potentially stopping us from experiencing and doing great things with our lives.

Would it be so unreasonable for you to begin to notice that while so many are becoming increasingly afraid of what they are watching and listening from the shore-line of their TV screens, papers, radio and internet sites of stories concerning financial ruin, fat cat salaries and bonuses, political intrigue and misdemeanour, huge share and job losses, murder and mayhem that it has the potential to become the norm, ie what we expect and believe our society is about.

Further, if we continue experiencing the media and their relentless' **'Breaking News on the hour, every hour'** stories, special reports and exclusives, telling us again and again that we are still on the edge, that governments across the globe such as Greece, Portugal, Spain and Italy and many more are running huge deficits that they haven't a hope in hell of clearing over the next decade, with a dark undertone that the fallout could spew out across Europe and affect us all, doesn't it become feasible, perhaps even reasonable that sooner or later we will begin to believe what they say? And if that's the case then it's more than plausible, wouldn't you agree, that at some point we will just begin filtering all information and all experience to confirm what we have seen and heard, and then go out and think, talk and act like it's all true.

To back this perception up can you remember early march 2008 when reports shifted across the pond to the USA as TV and internet screens lit up and screamed out to us that it was just getting worse, even as iconic financial giants such as Bear Stearn's Merchant Banking and Lehman Brothers investment Bank were going belly up, alongside the Washington Mutual, the biggest savings and loan association in the United States. Then as the WaMu was bought and shored up by the purchase of its banking operation by J P Morgan, more fear and uncertainty ensued. Even now as we move through 2010 and into 2011 the effects of this 'meltdown' are cascading down with Employment levels causing a near paralysis of fear as worried manufacturers in U.S. automobile, housing and the service sector cut back on production and manpower, whist at the same time worried consumers cut back on spending, further destabilising the biggest economy in the world. And even though latest figures show improvements it could get worse, much worse if we listen to the 'experts', with predictions that the credit crunch and recession may still be around in 2012, with millions more job losses around the world.

Today, as I write the U.K. Economy has just come out of recession with some forecasting models including that developed by the Credit Management Research Centre (CMRC) at Leeds University Business School, predicting that around 40,000 companies will have been declared insolvent in 2009. This represents a 35% increase on 2008 and a 62% increase since the end of 2007. (Although most commentators conveniently forget to mention that 500,000 new businesses will start up in 2009, with 60% of those start ups working from home)

Figures released by the Insolvency Service show corporate insolvencies rose to 4,941 in the first quarter of the year – an increase of 56 per cent on last year and up 7.1 per cent on the previous quarter.

Individual insolvencies also rose by 19 per cent on last year to 29,774 – the highest number since records began in 1960.

Personal bankruptcies soared by 23.4 per cent to 19,062 while individual voluntary arrangements (IVA's) under which individuals negotiate debt write-off deals with their creditors without a formal bankruptcy procedure were 11.8 per cent up on last year at 10,713.

Source: Times Online

At the same time the previous Labour government committed to borrowing and spending more and more money in order to spend its way out of the recession acknowledges that there must be drastic cuts as the UK faces a record budget deficit at approximately 12% of GDP rivalling that of the much troubled Greek economy. The problem is no-one can predict how this is going to work out, we are in uncharted waters...and it's the uncertainty of it all that fuels the speculation whilst the May 6th UK General Election returned the first hung parliament for 36 years with the resultant coalition government promising some of the biggest cuts ever seen in a comprehensive spending review.

I'm sure you'd agree that upon reading and listening to any of this continual selling and mass marketing of doom, gloom and bankruptcies while watching newsreels of people leaving work for the last time, unemployment heading upward and with iconic companies going bust virtually overnight, its true isn't it that continuously full colour, sensationalised and highly targeted 'breaking news', could seriously undermine your motivation and passion to begin and continue your big, big dream adventure.. because fear tends to have that power if allowed free reign.

The breaking news tells us that there is less and less money available in the economy due to an increasingly treacherous and uncertain banking terrain which, allegedly, is/was continuously under pressure from sub-prime mortgage defaults (mortgages given to those who could ill afford them, and who now find themselves in great difficulty paying the fees on those loans back to the banks.) Now, and although the money supply is easing, we are still informed that one of the underlying causes of the lack of money in the system is that the banks still have little confidence in one another, i.e. the Banks are afraid that if they lend there may still be some shocks within the system. I guess when whole economies can go into melt-down visa via Iceland and Greece, the pervading logic is that anything could still happen. Perhaps the recent Dubai default scare and the fear of a collapse of the Chinese housing bubble just stacks up the potential power of 'breaking news' events to derail us even further.

But wait; now hold on, because even after all this, I haven't even touched upon the four trillion dollar global cost of the credit crunch. Neither, have I mentioned the fall-out from rising food prices, or the oil, gas, nuclear and climate crisis plus the increasing dependency on Russia for energy supplies which could be/is problematic and may worsen at any time.

With the effects of these 'cataclysmic events' hitting us, or forecast to hit us sometime soon, you can see how, can you not, that if you follow the logic and the herd mentality through, then this is certainly no time for people to lift themselves up with the memorable maxim of 'Yes you Can', is it? And in the true logic of the reasonable dreamer, the very people who listen more to the negative influencers, it's just not a good time to start thinking big, bigger than you've ever allowed yourself to think before is it, nor to act on that big thinking, because the 'Breaking News' tells us it's about to get worse, so it must be true..mustn't it?

So listen, there's no money around, people are afraid for their jobs, afraid of failing as their security and values come under increasing threat, so why would you ever *begin now*? It's a crazy mentality isn't it, best 'wait 'til things pick up again' in a year to eighteen months, then you can take another look, that's the rational thing to do isn't it?

At the risk of repeating myself, it would be extremely unreasonable in these times would it not, to imagine any person, especially a growing, developing and confident inner winner, a big, big dreamer stepping up to the plate ahead of the crowd and seeing your future in big bright bold colours in stereo sound resonating and energising you as you work toward the brilliant future you truly want for yourself...I mean how likely is that in these 'most wretched of times'?

Yet let me stretch your imagination a little further because I couldn't believe any reasoned, rational person, I mean, you know, taking all the financials and economics together would dare to *trust in your gut instincts* and take a look at things through another set of lenses, perceiving another reality that says *I can do it*, and I can *start right now, could you.*

In reality, no matter what the breaking news says, you have to break the news down. Watch and listen carefully if you must, but don't get caught up in the hype, take what information you want or can leverage positively in your life and your big, big dream and use it. Look for facts instead of supposition and speculation. Question assertions and statements of fact by others by asking questions such as 'how do they know that?', or 'according to whom?' Or 'how does x automatically mean y, could it mean z instead, and what if it did, and how could I use that information today or tomorrow.

You see one of the absurdities of what and how you see and experience the breaking news is that you are so much more than the media think you are. You are the medium and the message, and almost certainly the only breaking news worth breaking is about you. Anything is possible for you when you have big, big dreams, and you can start right now on your pathway to achievement because most people have not even got out of bed to the opportunities contained within the relative pain and uncertainties. Many people really believe in the big breaking news stories and hold back, not giving their all for fear they will become another statistic.

Yet again we can see how this recession has been full of black holes, rent with paradoxical and ironic meaning as you begin to uncover with a curious and tenacious mindset, that other peoples' organisational, economic, social and cultural pain is your opportunity to heal. And what I mean by that is, as you no doubt know, where there is pain, lots of it, the world needs healers. So go out and commit to your incredible healing now. And remember to charge a reasonable margin.

Okay! So right now, it's very much make your mind up time, and I'd like to tell you the very best part of all of this. Are you ready to be dealt the ace in the pack? Do you love insider information? Are you listening very closely, because although I've been alluding to it, this is it, the cat out of the bag time, all the 'secrets of the big secret' rolled into one magnificent Havana (excuse the political incorrectness) and you know history has proved this secret, time and time again, hasn't it.) The fact is that the biggest single upside for you throughout all of this, and simultaneously the biggest single encouragement for you (with this information alone your about to get a ten-fold return on your purchased book price) is the hit-the-ground running, irrefutable truth that there is no better time for you to start now to *do what you love to do,* which means succeeding in making a healthy and wealthy living for yourself, because really there is so damn little competition around you, and even fewer with a big, big courageous attitude to laugh at and face down that scary monster, artificial barrier and two faced imposter called...the breaking news.

The Real Breaking News... Taking a peek inside the doors of perception

So what's really happening? As history repeats itself, and the media and marketing production lines hit fever pitch, projecting crippling uncertainties, paralysing fears and nose-diving economic and emotional instability, history is merely running the same reel one more time, showing us that it is the confident and daring dreamers, the courageous doers of the day who have always thrived in these times. It is they, *people like you*, who have always *found buyers for their compelling and remarkable big dreams and actions*, it is people like you who have forever drawn investors deep into their imagination and vision, and so my friend you have nothing to fear save for fear itself.

And imagine, you only need believe in yourself and your big, big dream and then go! Go now and Unleash your big, big dream upon the world because if it's all a stage anyway your presence has been requested and who are you to deny your audience your genius. Lastly, let me remind you who you really are, in all your abundance and glittering magnificence because it is within the miracle of your incredible mind, within your absolute uniqueness and soaring imagination that your big dreams reside. You are powered by a miracle of neural architecture, the like of which the planet has never experienced previously. As Science discovers more about how our brain functions we uncover facts that prove you are a miracle, a magnificent force of energy that has untapped reserves to call upon, and to this end it is worth knowing, repeating and acknowledging every day just what power you have at your fingertips to call on at any time, and wondrously, that power grows with use. This is your reality, so do it now and read the following paragraph at least seven times so it can become an imprint in your neuro-physiology and therefore benefit you every day of your life.

Throughout your life, the neural networks within your brain reorganize and reinforce themselves in response to new stimuli and learning experiences. This mind/body interaction is what stimulates brain cells to grow and connect with each other in the most complex of ways. They do so by extending branches of intricate nerve fibres called dendrites (from the Latin word for "tree"). These are the antennas through which neurons receive communication from each other. A healthy well-functioning neuron can be directly linked to tens of thousands of other neurons, creating a totality of more than a hundred trillion connections – each capable of performing 200 calculations per second! This is the structural basis of your brain's memory capacity and thinking ability. As a product of its environment, your "three pound universe" is essentially an internal map that reflects your external world.

#Source: The Franklin Institute Resources for Science Learning.

In other words, what your internal thinker thinks, your prover will generally create in your external reality. You really do have the power to create anything you desire. This potential doesn't just allow you to peek inside the doors of differing realities it blasts wide open the metaphorical and literal doors of perception for you (please take the time to read this one more time, slowly) as one begins to see the outer reality being created by the inner, so if you don't like what you see then by all means change it, if you do, then go ahead make it even better. And so when you put these facts about your brilliant mind into perspective who would deny that you can reach success in uncommon time, who would dare to say that you cannot create, discover and forge new openings and opportunities in better, more useful ways previously thought impossible for you. It's true isn't it that with *courage*, commitment and belief in oneself a person can prove these times to be the best of times as they fast become the defining moments of your life so far. Now isn't that something worth celebrating.

So which is it to be, the magnificent adventurer riding wave after wave upon the shorelines of your big dreams, or one of reading and listening to the media and other people with vested interests sending out defeat inducing fears of debt, ruin and unemployment, leading only to a path of restlessness, discontent and endless replays of your glory days, days of what might have been, could have been and should have been.

But Listen! Isn't it great! You're not going down that path of if only... and so, where will you be in five, or ten or twenty years. It's time to take a look ahead to decide where you want to be and with whom. To positively plan, break into constituent parts and act on your vision, decisions, passion and belief with an all consuming commitment to achieving your big, big dreams.

"I have had dreams and I have had nightmares, but I have conquered my nightmares because of my dreams"

Dr Jonas Salk

A Pure Adrenalin Rush

So for you, when you have big big dreams, turning them into an unstoppable source of energy and passion becomes less about the dream itself and more about you the person, your purpose, values and the drive behind the big dream. Your big, big dream energy enables you, makes you solid, right down the middle, irresistible, immovable...hungry, starving and ravenous for achievement and success. Hungry like...for the last taste of food you'll ever have. The last drop of water you'll ever drink.

Yes, you've got to want it that badly and then some more. It is worth remembering now that you are the image of the dreamer, the magnificent dreamer of the day that T.E. Lawrence (Lawrence of Arabia) wrote of when describing you as 'a dangerous man or woman, because you are not like the dreamers of the night who dream their dreams in the dusty recesses of their minds only to wake in the day to find all was vanity. No, you are dangerous because you act upon your dreams with eyes wide open in order to make them possible, to make them come alive.

Turning your big dreams into reality means you are consumed with a sense of confidence in your destiny, that come what may, you will not be denied. Like a pure adrenalin rush coursing through your veins, you are unchained, unlimited and untameable like the very *Rapids of the Niagara* River which carries some of the most dangerous rapids in the world.

There is in fact a striking similarity to the dangerous nature of the rapids and your own very dangerous and challenging ability to make things happen, which can often bring with it an uncomfortable and oddly disconcerting sense of uncertainty to those who know or at least thought that they knew you.

It's a truism isn't it that big dreams arrive early and without warning, usually born in the very early years of life and often crystallising in the teenage years. It has been said that the roots of big dreams develop maybe as young as seven, eight or nine years of age, or perhaps even earlier. One certainty and something that is essential that you come to know and understand is that your greatest dreams come with a price as they can, and often will, take you through a roller coaster ride of emotional, mental and physical pain, perhaps via the lowest points of your life before leading you to your destiny. (And no success guru will ever tell you that cold reality)

It is in truth, a fatal mistake to believe confidence and dreams are achieved without vision, a workable plan, perseverance and hard work and also without pain, fear and rejection. It is naive in the extreme to think that without struggle and sweat, both emotional and physical that you can succeed. You will have to put the grease-ball overalls on just like Thomas Edison who said that genius is 99% sweat and 1% inspiration, and then be ready to change into the finest of suits you can afford in order to sell your big dream, whilst in-between (and often simultaneously) enduring a level of doubt, pain, discomfort, un-ease and dis-ease, to a point where those with just a vague goal, a whispy, dreamy flimsy whisper in the night kind of dream, would sooner give up and settle for much less than who they are. But let me re-assure you that this is where the confidence and the resilience come from, they come from the realisation that your destiny is truly in the best of hands, that you can survive the storms of rejection and perceived failure, that you are not an imposter and that you and dreams will most certainly not unravel.

"Dream Big Dreams, imagine yourself doing the greatest thing in the world"

Barack Obama

It's a given, a natural turn of events, that going after your big, dreams and taking consistent actions makes for difficult and often challenging personal relationships because making your big dreams come true demands so much of you and from others, often testing the limits of their faith understanding and love for you. One can find one's self in a state of continually asking for the right to justify and negotiate each spectre of time that you give, so that the people who deserve the best of your limited time...get it. It is never that you don't want to give of yourself; it's just so challenging and uncomfortable to explain to others, that you are on a unique journey, an adventure to the moon, the sun and the stars...to the solar system, a journey to the very epicentre of life itself...and so you must prepare now for when this time arrives, for arrive it will and you must be ready to protect and preserve your most prized relationships.

And yet still every day you, the achiever, writer, producer and director at large must wake up empowered, driven by that pure adrenalin rush, emboldened to take massive and confident action to succeed, in spite of what may or may not have happened yesterday or the day or week before, be it rejection, put downs, slap downs, emotional highs and lows, little or no money or resources, because after all, without the bitterness nothing would ever again taste so sweet. You have made a decision and you will not be denied. It is said that the difference between achievers and non-achievers is that achievers are willing to do whatever it takes in order to succeed. To that end you say...*So be it.*

For winners like you now, time has lost its sense of power within the explosive and irresistible nature of your big dreams, for you are a natural born winner, a survivor and thriver. If this were not so you and the species as a whole would not have adapted and survived. You have inherited strategies for survival and success proven over millions of years, passed on by your ancestors, you have learnt to adapt to changing environments or simply disappear. And so this period of time, coupled with the ensuing financial and economic situation, presents an almost unprecedented combination of circumstances for you to fulfill your greatest of dreams, as you find yourself continuing to do whatever is deemed necessary to take you forward and toward your destiny.

"Most people never run far enough on their first wind to find out they've got a second. Give your dreams all you've got and you'll be amazed at the energy that comes out of you"

William James

People, some good and some bad but, significantly mostly good, find themselves attracted to you and your big, big dreams because of your boundless energy and love for life itself, and this despite almost everyone around you bemoaning the economic, social or political situation as some sort of awful pre-determined intervention. People are becoming irresistibly drawn to you as you squeeze every droplet of life as though it has been borrowed and you are tasked with using your talents for good, for gain and a defining purpose. You can be confident now, big dream achiever, as you are reminded of the story of the good and faithful servant in the parable of the talents, in which the story tells of a master who upon leaving his home to travel gave his three servants differing amounts of money.

On returning from his travels, the master asks his servants for an account of the money given to them. The first servant reported that he was given five talents, and he had made five talents more. The master praised the servant as being good and faithful, and gave him more responsibility because of his faithfulness, and invited the servant to be joyful together with him. The second servant said that he had received two talents, and he had made two talents more. The master praised this servant in the same way as being good and faithful, giving him more responsibility and inviting the servant to be joyful together with him.

The last servant who had received one talent reported that knowing his master was a hard man; he buried his talent in the ground for safekeeping and therefore returned the original amount to his master. The master called him a wicked and lazy servant saying that he should have placed the money in the bank to generate interest. The master commanded that the one talent be taken away from that servant, and given to the servant with ten talents, because everyone that has much will be given more, and whoever that has a little, even the little that he or she has will be taken away.

And so, burning up with passion, a sense of purpose and commitment you are on your way to becoming recognised as someone with a sense of meaning, of timing, a person who gets things done. You're smart enough to know that making one brave leap toward your big dream, though awesome in and of itself will never be enough, that you must take your big dream and break it down into the most manageable of chunks. Breaking it down, you can clearly see, hear and feel the path before you as each stone marks the next benchmark, the next sign post on your way. I would like to say Realistic chunks as most of the self help genre state...but for me I cannot commit to the realistic because often the next step demands a leap of faith and where is the realism in that? measureable and achievable I say yes because you are making your dreams come true and anybody smart enough and brave enough is hanging onto your shirt tails for the ride, doing the best they can to help you through each step of the way and so much more becomes achievable because people know there is a good chance you will help their own big dreams come true in the process. You live life literally and metaphorically in overdrive as the creative juices are flowing, and flowing 24/7.

    You exhibit the very nature of a winner which means that you don't, no can't sleep, until you fall asleep... anywhere. It may be in the theatre, a cinema, a restaurant, a car, a sofa, quite literally anywhere, like a babe in a mother's arms...

    Burning up with a love of life itself often a person like you can't speak quickly enough, as you try in vain to keep up with the pictures and images ricocheting through your mind. You can't talk fast enough as the sounds and ideas whistle past you at the speed of light, all but throwing you to the floor. Your emotions are so raw you find the very art of concealment alien, but you are learning so quickly now, are you not? You are now growing in confidence as a continuous learner, curious, alert and aware... the decision made, an inner winner, having won the first battle, the battle for the inner mind, you are now moving onto the creation of all things on the physical plane and you know, do you not, that it's all wide open with all to play for.

    If you were to play, just play with your imagination as a child for a moment, can you create a movie where you are fast becoming the sun, the moon and the sky, as you see, hear, feel and breathe your way into the greatest of dreamers, thinkers and achievers of the past, present and future. It may be an Einstein, or a Kennedy, a Churchill, a Da Vinci, an Ali or Michelangelo. It could be Caravaggio or maybe a Golda Meir, Eva Peron, a Mother Theresa, an Oprah or even Barack Obama... the list is endless and different for everyone. Yet all of these great people have one thing in common – they are all winners, big, big dream achievers. Whether they describe themselves as such or not – they are creative, action-driven people – they may feel or have felt afraid, but never lacked the courage to face down fear and failure, because they understood that, as part of life, part of becoming successful, a true big, big dreamer, needs to fail again and again, to keep on learning and getting up, keep coming back time after time after time. Karl Jung the great Swiss Psychiatrist wrote of the collective unconscious as a process whereupon we may tap into 'a reservoir of the experience of our species', a greater wisdom than we yet own...so who are you tapping into, whose wisdom are you drawing upon now as you think about it, and whose wisdom might you draw upon knowing this.

"You see things; and you say, why? But I dream things that never were; and I say, why not?"

George Bernard Shaw

Growing in confidence through action, feedback and more action, winners, big dream achievers like you learn from experience, from others, from history and by example. You move forward by continually thinking outside of the box, in fact for winners like you there is not one box, but multiple boxes...no one cake but multiple cakes, enough for everyone. No longer deterred and not for long weighed down by the vagaries and uncertainties of life, you are developing a growing self-belief that offers a sense of certainty that you can come through and will come through anything.

Perhaps you are penniless, bankrupt or homeless, or worse or maybe none of these and yet often the more the pain the greater the reason to make things happen. Because whether you consider yourself poor or not, that is no longer the point, no longer the perspective as you already begin to realise quite naturally that you are unlimited in resources, natural, physical and universal, and this economic storm has just become perfect for you to unleash your uniqueness, ingenuity strength and magnificence. Your adrenalin is flowing which in turn means you are becoming unstoppable.

"There are two ways to live; you can live as if nothing is a miracle; you can live as if everything is a miracle"

Albert Einstein

And remember, as I alluded to earlier, all of this whether you acknowledge it or not, originated from a very young age as first thoughts, feelings and words came together and you were just beginning to find your feet. You may or may not have felt differently from everyone else, because you couldn't articulate what had already begun, as a young winner only just beginning to touch and reach out to your as yet unexplored and unexplained canvas. You recognise now that the confidence, belief, mistakes and learning necessary to walk and talk was never explained to you, but undeterred you didn't wait around for anyone or anything, determined, you just went for it, got a result and went again, learnt some and then went again and again... before eventually succeeding.

The very early character of the dream achiever, always a work under construction, has at first little idea how to deal with failure, rejection, pain and confusion or the ebbing of confidence as fleeting unstoppable and winning moments are captured in early life only to seemingly escape, albeit temporarily; recovering later often much later in life, as one discovers time has no relevance to the focused action driven dreams of the winner and big dream achiever.

Your Magnificent Vision

"Dreams pass into the reality of action. From the actions stems the dream again; and this interdependence produces the highest form of living"
Anais Nin

Visionary, (optimistic often in the extreme) determined and hugely persistent – these are just some of the character traits that are beginning to set you apart. Right now maybe you're just living in and for the moment your dreams come true and you've made it, done it, gone on to become a leader for a new generation, maybe a painter, a poet an artist, perhaps a new one in a million author like J.K. Rowling. Or perhaps you're discovering and creating a new or hybrid model of the biggest and best of the social media, perhaps your big, big dreams are about becoming the greatest footballer on the planet, better than Ronaldo, Kaka, Rooney or even a Messi of Barcelona. What if you were to become the lead singer with the biggest band in the world or the next Valentino Rossi, a Wayne Gretzky, Hillary Clinton or Barack Obama? And still the big dreams grow and grow because maybe you want to be the next great explorer of the mind, of genius and our planet, in the mould of a Karl Jung, Christopher Columbus or Captain James Cook or maybe Hernan Cortes, the Spanish adventurer and explorer, perhaps a discoverer of things never seen or thought of before. Or, could it be you want to be a better athlete than Michael Jordon or Tiger Woods, or a brilliant and revolutionary designer like Sir James Dyson, the much missed Alexander McQueen or aVivien Westwood, perhaps a Miuccia Prada, or a brilliant entertainer like Madonna, Lady Ga Ga, Missy Elliot or a Beyonce. What about becoming the successor to Damien Hurst, or someone like or maybe totally different to Andy Warhol or a Jackson Pollock? Maybe you're big, big dream is to become a Billionaire like Branson, Oprah, a Larry Page and Sergey Brin of Google or maybe Steve Jobs or Facebook creator Mark Zuckerberg?

Truly anything is possible because after Barack 'nothing is impossible'. Impossible is just a word to the inner winner, you can be anything or anyone you choose to be, metaphorically and literally all things become possible. So begin now. Be unique and astonishing with something remarkable to offer the world. The personality, creed and colour of dream achievers may be manifold and yet they all have two things in common, they never

ever give up on themselves and they believe in the power of their vision to drive forward change. It is the energy within your dreams that exudes life, as it becomes the provider-in-chief of your sustenance, the food, the sun, water and air to your grasping, gasping, twitching, reaching-for-the-stars, needy and brilliant inner self. For dream achievers, becoming even more joyful, happy, values driven, super successful and often as a by-product, rich beyond your greatest dreams, constitutes the very hope and essence of your life. There is nothing else to get up or lay down for. If you doubt me, and if you dare, I ask you to explore the frenetic, adventurous and electrified vision and lives of the then teenage dreamer, such as Bill Gates (Microsoft) 'I want to put a PC on the table of every household', or Richard Branson, 'I want Virgin to be as well known around the world as Coca Cola', or Steve Jobs (Apple) 'I want to put a dent in the universe', and Michael Dell (Dell Computers) 'I want to work directly with customers and provide them with the latest computing technology, custom built to their needs'.

Or maybe you might want to get curious about the vision and hopes of someone less famous but equally courageous such as Bonita Norris who at twenty two years of age became the youngest British woman ever to climb Mount Everest in 2010. Or how about the oldest woman ever to climb Mount Everest, Anna Czerwinska who at age 50 climbed Everest from the Nepal side at the dawn of the new millennium. What vision, passion and purpose drove this amazing woman to conquer this Monster of a Mountain at 29029 feet or 8848 metres...the world's highest mountain peak

"Yes, I am a dreamer. For a dreamer is one who can find his way by moonlight, and see the dawn before the rest of the world"

Oscar Wilde

Or even, just ask your son, your daughter, your nephew or niece, a friend, a friend of a friend because I promise you this much...you will never have to look far for the action driven dream achiever, because like the myriad of birds that soar toward the sky there are millions of big dream achievers all across the globe...hoping, praying, smiling, laughing crying, acting on miracles...just living, playing out their often stunning, outrageous, brilliant and unrestrained futures in the theatre of their minds and upon the world.

You know, maybe a big dream pulsating achiever is sitting not so far away from you right now as you read this, and just stretching your imagination just a little bit more, what if it's always been so much more simple than it ever appeared to our limited perceptions because perhaps we have always known that the big dream achiever resides much closer to home than we ever realised. Yet there's something about right now isn't there, about timing, about a sense of urgency and about momentum. About not hanging around anymore 'til it's all gone...you know, like stopping the energy being sucked out of us by the boring everydayness of life. Yet we can never escape or ignore, and neither should we want to, the cold stark reality that for every boy or girl, man or woman who dares to dream, only one out of so many, many, will ever get to kiss the sky and live the dream, but it's still worth the decision, still worth the commitment to follow and play to a different drum, our very own drum because of what it makes of us upon the journey.

Many will leave the dream behind, for something less than whom they are. Still others will lose themselves, imploding and all but surrendering to the uncertain winds and vagaries of life, financial, emotional or otherwise. We have to realise that all determined, big dream achievers suffer the inner turmoil and volcanic swings and fallout from battered and broken dreams, dreams that seemingly must first prove their value through searing and burning coals before fulfilment. Yet remember this as you contrast different realities...the world consists of two kinds of dreamer, Dreamers of the night, who will never ever see their dreams fulfilled, never get to the mountain top and who are left seeking consolation by playing out their lives in a plastic fifteen minute celebrity culture, all the while, hopelessly living in quiet cold desperation, as Thoreau put it. And just think, then there is you the dreamer and doer of the day, and you're not a dreamer of the night...isn't that an amazing!!

"The key to happiness is having dreams; the key to success is making them come true"

James Allen

Don't just dream it – Do it now

On becoming unreasonable...

Just before you become fully aware of how far you have come and how close you are to becoming everything you can be, and while you begin to recognise the internal attitude and belief that is propelling you toward the achievement of your biggest dreams, let's take the opportunity to remind ourselves, lest we forget, that history replicates the stories of millions of ordinary dreamers' aka reasonable dreamers of the night every day of our lives. This happens right in front of you on your TV screens or on your social websites and networks, such as Face Book, Twitter and You Tube plus any other medium you care to name, right across the planet. People, young and older desperately reaching out to someone or something...trying to connect, searching for a tribe or group of people who are like them and who can offer them something that compensates for not having or not acting on their big, big dreams. When you look with a careful eye and with a curious and hungry mind, then you will come across clues throughout this book and your life leading you toward the development of the character, the powerful beliefs and attitudinal DNA of achievers of big dreams.

To recap and just so we keep on track...we now know that at first big dreams are stories and signs of wonderwall, of Camelot, of a wonderful synergistic dance with triumph, pathos and mythology all rolled into one. Captured within a brief moment in time, the reasonable dreams of the dreamer of the night take the form of seeming reality until the inevitable failure or rejection occurs. There then seems to follow some kind of fight back, a first intuitive refusal of defeat...this is maybe wired into all dreamers. Already we know it's not going to be easy, but we are generally ignorant of the first visible signs of this fact that some form of failure or rejection is inevitable, (and required!!!) and that you are going to have to find a way back. The unpalatable reality for many is that the millions and millions of 'reasonable, ordinary night dreams' are whimsical, fantasist and lack the compelling power, energy and irresistibility of a winner's dreams. And so the ordinary dreamer comes to accept five beliefs:

Five destructive beliefs of an ordinary dreamer

1. Failure is what I expected anyway

2. My dream wasn't real, never was, never will be

3. I'm not good enough, never will be...they were right!

4. I need to suppress this pain (unconscious thoughts)

5. I needed to listen to reason and reality and get over my childish dreams, get a job or a trade or something.

You know that ordinary dreamers (dreamers of the night) have never thought as George Bernard Shaw did when stating 'that people who get on in this world are the people who get up and look for the circumstances they want and if they can't find them, they make them'. Instead ordinary dreamers walk away from challenge, failure and rejection not understanding the real and unbridled opportunity held within each event.

They bemoan their bad luck, their bad genes, their paucity and poverty thinking attitude and finances, whilst refusing to believe that how they choose to think about their life and the meaning they give to any situation is what they get in reality and is hugely influencing what they will attempt to do and any future success.

Truly a key factor is, to what extent people believe their achievement is influenced by their external environment, rather than their internal environment. That is, their ability to influence what they experience and thus their actions with their thoughts feeling and words. Things have never happened, nor ever will happen by sitting around thinking things better or waiting for other people to make it happen for you, you've got to do it yourself now.

Too often the reasonable dreamers' internal experience is punctuated by an air of negativity and sense of uncertainty. It is here we find the first clues to the separation and decoding of an ordinary and reasonable dreamer compared to the unreasonable, remarkable and dynamic big dream achiever.

"Champions aren't made in the gyms. Champions are made from something they have deep inside them – a desire, a dream, a vision"

Muhammad Ali

Winners...
The Ultimate DNA

1. Big Dreamers are winners. Often unreasonable and unrealistic, they will not accept any circumstances that get in their way or prevent them moving forward. They are constantly asking unreasonable questions both of themselves and of other successful big dreamers and preparing to act on those answers. Seeing things from different angles, shades, possibilities they are ready to devour opportunities which appear, and to the unreasonable big dreamer, opportunity will appear, it's never ever a question of if, much more a question of when, where, what and how to take advantage when it (or they) do appear. Ordinary dreamers of the night are incredibly reasonable, stuck in an early schooling mentality, an attitude (often unspoken) that says dreams are not for you that success is all down to luck, chance and who you know. It seems like they are unaware of the positive power and persuasion of physical and mental movement, of passion and persistence, of continually

meeting people face to face in negotiation and other advanced learning situations.

2. Big dreamers are unreasonable. They are Action driven people, they understand that without a map to guide one's journey a person does not have any real and substantive idea of where they are heading. The big, big dreamer understands from role models, mentors experience and learning that it is much better to have a torch to guide you in the dark than to wander about in a vague hope that you will reach your destination. So they plan ahead knowing that the map they hold in their head is not the territory and that the terrain they travel will change from that internal map and so flexibility will be a tool of choice and necessity.

Ordinary dreamers have no action plan for achievement, and those that do have, design it on a foundation of inflexibility and poor beliefs about failure and road blocks ahead, they have no conviction deep down within that says '**I will succeed no matter what**'. It goes without saying there is no follow through with necessary and often unpalatable actions that successful big dreamers carry out consistently.

The truth is that ordinary dreamers will not do what action driven big dreamers do every day on a consistent basis.

The Mantra Of The Big, Big Dreamer:

"People are always blaming circumstances for what they are. I don't believe in circumstances. The people who get on in this world are the people who get up and look for the circumstances they want and if they can't find them, make them"
George Bernard Shaw

3. Big Dreamers persist through all 'blocks' (clue... there are no blocks, it's how you interpret those blocks and the meaning you give them) using their senses to scan, monitor and compare how far they have come since last month, last week...yesterday. If they are off course they change what they are doing in order to get back on course. Big dreamer winners like you are acutely aware of the cause/effect/meaning implications of their actions as they look ahead to the consequences and impact of their important moves. They watch and listen, feeling their way through changing, potentially dangerous environments asking questions and seeking answers from inside and outside, from others who have already been there.

   Ordinary dreamers don't develop an attitude of persistence; they rarely experience the winning post as getting nearer and nearer. They will usually stop and not attempt again after a small number of rejections or setbacks. How many times have you heard the excuse 'I ran out of money', or 'I ran out of time', or 'it was just bad timing/luck/? The fact is the Big Dream achiever says **it is exactly because** of the credit crunch/recession/downturn that I am making my dreams a reality and when they need to, they remember the famous anecdote of the great golfer Gary Player when asked if his form was down to luck he replied 'You know it's funny, the harder I practice, the luckier I seem to get'.

4. Big dreamers are remarkable. They act out of remarkable principles, they know they must develop a disciplined way of life if they are to achieve their dreams, yet manage keep an extraordinary level of flexibility to work with other people, opportunity and risk when the need arises.

Ordinary dreamers never learn about nor realise just what it takes in terms of discipline, organisation and efficiency in order to succeed. They rarely adopt an everyday attitude of 'get out there 'n meet 'em 'n greet 'em' philosophy to life and success. They don't imagine that it's possible to achieve extraordinary breakthroughs and new deals, just by asking some unreasonable questions of unreasonably successful winners. They, ordinary dreamers, will never recognise the fact that most winners in life want you to succeed and will do whatever is possible for them to do in order to help.

5. Big dream achievers have outrageous, compelling and lip smacking dreams, with plans and processes that chunk those big dreams down into workable and achievable steps to success.

    Ordinary dreamers never learn to use the power of setting big goals, breaking them down into measurable and achievable performance tasks, and as a consequence never empower, refuel or energise themselves enough each day to win life's big challenges

6. Big dreamers are winners, always looking for the best people to work with, people who are smarter than them, people who can add value to the dream, the product, the service, operation and company.

    Ordinary dreamers have little knowledge of the passion and vision that attracts and builds up a high quality team of believers, 'sneezers' and achievers around them that can considerably shorten the journey to big dream achievement.

7. Big and successful dreamers know there is always more to gain from the failures than the successes and so continue to plough a field through any event or scenario, always looking for different outcomes and

alternative meanings to outcomes that will help keep them moving forward. This is a skill. They have a willingness to look, listen and learn from constructive criticism and act on advice if perceived as correct.

Ordinary dreamers are unaware of the organic nature of the opportunities that arise, ie that there is always more than one pathway or strategy in which to reach their destination. They rarely understand that the clues to success lay in their failures, within their imagination, courage, creativity and responses and so avoid the relative pain of failure and criticism that has to occur in order to learn and succeed.

8. Big Dreamers are winners in the game of life and never settle for second best, until they have given their all. If they have given a 100% then they are able to recognise there is nothing more they can do and so detach from outcome. They acknowledge they have given their very best, having squeezed every last bit of juice out of the fruit, they move on, having little time for regrets, besides they have too much to do.

They realise that the success comes from the extraordinary adventure that is this life, and from the incredible discoveries about themselves that no ordinary dreamer will ever encounter.

Ordinary dreamers are full of regret and remorse over lost time, lost money, and relationships never realising that they were always at a choice point in which they could move toward some other life or adventure that was perhaps more suited for them. They never question the prospect of developing another dream, and it is not hard to see how life for an ordinary dreamer can drift into one of existential angst or stress. It's not difficult to see the onset of mental and emotional health challenges as the ordinary dreamer becomes wracked by questions and later guilt about why they 'failed', and who was to blame, and where to now?

And so it is my belief that the keys to achieving big, big dreams lay within you. That today we are at a crossroads whereupon we can really choose to be unreasonable, opposite thinking big dreamers that can win and win big, by having and developing seriously juicy and compelling big dreams that will provide fuel for the journey. Because as tough as the realities people face in a post credit crunch and recession-led culture, a dream is made ordinary by not being of a compelling, dynamic and attractive nature, and therefore it is unable to survive a battering by undeniable realities and a media that lives and breathes on crisis and sensationalism. People may want to remember that the media's raison d'être is to sell copy and unfortunately, nothing sells like misery, gloom and despondency, that says 'cut back, draw in, protect what you have because look, bad times are out there and they're coming after you.

Yet when you've got big dreams you continue taking unreasonable actions that are more powerful than fear. This is not to say that big dreamers have no fears, it's just that they learn to live with them and use the energy to move forward rather than reverse. Remember winners, don't ever quit, ever.

*"Twenty years from now you will be more disappointed by the things that you didn't do than by the ones you did do. So throw off the bowlines. Sail away from the safe harbour. Catch the trade winds in your sails.
Explore. Dream. Discover"*

Mark Twain

Become Irresistible...
because there's just so little competition

You must take on a form of irresistibility. Ultimately it's not your environment or circumstances that lead you into decline, it is the inability to call on the physiological and psychological beliefs, attitude, resources and the support to change your circumstances, so they fit the picture of your dreams.

You must listen and apply knowledge and thought alongside every day positive and unreasonable actions, making friends with figures of influence who are a part of, and apart from your own inner circle. You must do whatever is necessary and legitimate to get that first foot in the door. To be prepared to start at the bottom, just as Paul Arden the advertising Genius and author would say 'hang around the place you want to be, go make the tea and expect no payment – all of a sudden people get used to you, you become one of them...'. Mmmm! Maybe that's just too deliciously simplistic for us...isn't it?

Remember none of this is easy; it's very simple but not easy. If it was then every dream would come true and there would be a pony in every young girl's back garden. Dreams must be worked and worked hard with enthusiasm every day, but most of all worked smart, with attitude and self-belief in order to become irresistible. You must become irresistible and unreasonable all at once in what you do, how you do it and to what lengths you will go in order to create the circumstances that build unstoppable momentum.

Donald Trump has said on more than one occasion that momentum is so important to success that if you lose it your crash can be spectacular. Momentum is acutely important to irresistibility. Understanding how you become irresistible and build momentum is a little like Tim Ferris says in his great book The 4-hour work week. 'From contacting Billionaires to rubbing shoulders with celebrities – it's as easy as believing it can be done. I guess you've heard the old chestnut of how lonely it is at the top haven't you, but did you also know why that's the case? Well the reason is because ninety nine percent of people in the world are convinced they are incapable of achieving great things, so they aim for mediocrity, the middle or lower ground. It's true.

Therefore, a useful reality to believe is that the level of competition is thus fiercest for the middle ground, for realistic goals. So really it's not that lonely at the top, it's just that there is so much more room there. I'm stating specifically that in our culture people generally expect you to fail, expect you to fall down and not continually get up when the going gets tough? Why is that do you think? Because in the main that is what everyone else does. They'll say 'of course it's good and normal to dream when you're a child, but then you have to grow up, you need to get realistic, accept life is hard and not fair and that's what dreams are, wishes, that only the lucky few achieve' and crucially, (here comes the implicit message) you are not one of the lucky few. It's just too hard, so you'll need to deal with the disappointment by having a trade behind you. But the reality is that that is B.S. - always has been and always will be.

Giant Characteristics...
of Big, Big Dreamers

Reach for the stars and begin with the end in mind. This is the starting point where you begin to turn the dream into one of unstoppable power. We now know through successful big dreamers of the past and the present and via an amazing methodology of attitude and experimentation called Neuro-linguistic programming, created by Dr Richard Bandler and John Grinder in the early 1970's, which studies and models the beliefs, strategies and physiology of successful people, that success leaves footprints, leaves explicit and implicit characteristics.

Therefore, as an example, in order for you to give yourself the best chance of success you need to totally immerse yourself within your compelling dream and in someone you would like to emulate or become better than. For example running your own successful business or playing for the most successful club side in the world, at this time Barcelona, would require of course a natural talent, but talent in and of itself is never enough in business, sport or any worthwhile big dream endeavour. You would need to focus on what you wanted as if already a reality, you are the finished article as you begin to laser in with emotional intensity as you see yourself (as if already part of the team) in a Barcelona shirt because you already know how important the motto is to the Catalans, hence you remember the meaning of '"Mes que un club" (More than a club).

Playing with Lionel Messi and the rest of the players on the luscious green turf of the massive 98,000 capacity Nou Camp stadium, you are in the dressing room listening to the manager, Josep 'Pep' Guardiola taking everything in, hearing the incredible noise levels from inside the stadium as it gets louder and louder, richer and richer in your mind's eye and inner ear.

And now you hear the Nou Camp fans calling your name. All this whilst looking through your own eyes, seeing who would be around you and what they would look like, what are they saying and doing? Now you know what the beliefs, mental strategies and physical traits of the mega successful are because you are one of them. What are you saying to yourself now you are a star? What are your team mates saying to you and how does that make you feel.

And once you recognise it is not the stardom per se that you want but the feelings of being a Barcelona player, then you can recognise that you have what it takes to be an inner winner as the DNA of success becomes installed into your neurology, and the good feelings inside of your imagination become the place where you find the drive, energy, power and determination to keep going for your dream. So, if we uncover that it's the feelings of being successful that we want, not the fact of being successful, then why wait? take the feelings of being very successful and bring them back into the present. Aren't you going to be more resourceful than ever before?

Tips for the top

1. **Prepare for Success**
    Act as if your dream is already achieved and truly believe in it becoming your destiny. Absorb your future surroundings like a sponge, while acting as if you are already successful, then you can become inspired to take the day-to-day actions necessary to become who you desire most of all. Act as if you know the way forward, act as if any obstacle, objection or rejection is just part of an inevitable learning curve you must conquer and utilise in order to reach the summit of your biggest dreams.

2. **Believe with all your heart in the integrity and validity of your dream.**
    If the dream was not in your heart and soul you would not desire it so. The word De-Sire comes from the Latin meaning "of the Father," to mean that it is of Spirit ... so validate, appreciate and respect that part of you that loves you so much that it has created something so wonderful and remarkable in your life.

3. **Read, listen, watch, experience. Ask questions of your role model in action. Watch how your heroes think and act. Listen out for the beliefs and thinking strategies of your role model, especially the very successful ones, as they write about themselves or at the very least have books ghost-written for them.**

4. They give interviews about how they think about winning, losing, failure and rejection and about quitting. How they grew up and overcame disappointment, perceived failure and rejection and still never gave up, and you know they will come up with one or two nuggets of pure gold for you to hold onto and leverage into your own actions and beliefs, characteristics that can accelerate your journey, and remember this, no matter what you hear, see or are told, they are accessible to the determined person, a person just like you. So Soak up how your hero is willing to take a different perspective than anyone else, how they are able to make up any belief that supports their big dreams.

   Success is do-able, possible and probable. You are already wonderful, remarkable beyond imagination and as you shift your thinking and beliefs to match this miracle called you to your daily actions, you will begin to find your authentic and successful self.

BELIEFS...The leverage to Success

Your beliefs will determine what you can and can't do and even what you will attempt to do in your life. Beliefs affect your behaviours, your capabilities, your ability to adapt to life with new ways of seeing and doing things. They filter what we learn and how quickly we learn. Beliefs that you have come to rely upon over the years as being true about you, in the sense that they expose your perceived limitations, couldn't be further away from the truth, because your beliefs are not you. Nor were they created when you were born or somehow became a brilliant decision by you to fit your life around. At least that's a generalisation on my part anyway.

    My perception is that our beliefs were formed partly in childhood and re-enforced during puberty and early adulthood. I think our beliefs about ourselves that we carry around with us were encouraged consciously and unconsciously by our parents, peers, teachers, culture, outcomes and results, also by our decisions, failures and the meanings we attached to any event ie 'I failed the English test which means I'll never by any good with English Language, which also means that I'll need to be on my guard (defensive) when I'm around educated people'. Or, 'I've only ever earned minimum wages so why should I go for my big dreams of becoming something more'? Remember our beliefs are not true per se they are only generalisations, perceptions or ideas about something or someone. They give us a sense of certainty, but they are not certainties. The give us a way of organising information into some coherent structure, but that still doesn't make them true. And if they are not true, then how important a breakthrough could that discovery be? It is important to learn and understand especially for the natural winner, that what we perceive as reality is not real; it's just one version of events based on how we are thinking and feeling at that moment, a set of ingrained, comfortable and habitual ways of thinking, a precept ie a set of instructions or rules that we are used to living by, rules which inform our decisions about what we can or will not do.

The version that we used to operate from went like this didn't it...What we see, hear, feel and say to ourselves is true, there is no other reality other than that which we experience, and I accept those limitations. Another reality, and one that action driven Big Dreamers live by, sometimes at first uncomfortably, goes like this (and it is here a person can gain the real leverage to success) that what we see, hear, feel and say to ourselves is not necessarily true and is not the only reality, it's just one descriptive programme that I can change if I wish. Steven Covey of 'seven principles of highly effective people' fame, rightly states 'I am not defined by my past but by my imagination', and thus our mental and emotional models of what can be, of what we can achieve are massively strengthened via our imagination. So we can acknowledge that what's really been going on is that from a very early age we became bombarded with information from the external environment with millions of bits of information thrown at us every minute. In order that we stay sane and prevent ourselves from falling victim to information overload we perform a sanity-saving exercise upon ourselves by filtering, distorting and generalising information so it fits in with what's real for us. As we now know what is real for us is influenced by our past experience, memories, decisions and traumas, and by people close to us such as parents, peers and role models (good and bad), so what we come to believe about ourselves is heavily influenced by our experience of life. That is why we say the map is not the territory. For instance a map of the city of London cannot be representative of London itself, because it cannot possibly show the terrain itself or the smells and sounds, therefore the map becomes useful if it is an accurate representation only. Similarly, what we used to believe about ourselves no longer has to define who we are because the belief is just a description that at one time may or may not have been useful for us to act upon.

We are so much more than our past experience and how we currently perceive and limit ourselves. A person can try on different beliefs every day and see what fits. ie the belief that you are going to have an awesome day doesn't necessarily mean you will, but what it does mean is that you are going to give yourself the best opportunity to make that happen by believing that the day will be awesome. What happens is that you start at an unconscious level to filter all information to fall in line with the belief, whilst finding yourself doing things that help shape the day to be awesome, and in particular, awesome for you. Did you know that research has proved that creative people are creative precisely because they believe they are creative, which means that what works for your heroes can work for you because all neurology works the same. So what they can do you can replicate.

Read, listen, watch and experience your heroes and role models achieving their dreams. Absorb how specifically they are making things happen (and importantly, how they are maintaining them) and what daily action steps they are taking.

Go ahead and ask them and when you find out go out and do the same things. Make your dreams and goals consistent with your beliefs and values, what is truly important to you. Be in control of your beliefs and make them work as leverage to lift you when you need access to all your resources, rather than have them work against you. Live the art of the unreasonable dreamer, believe that anything is possible and go out and win, and win big. Our beliefs about ourselves, our environment and our ability to change things around are that powerful. So to you big dream achiever, creator of big, big dreams that only a child can dream...choose your beliefs well.

Lest you forget our beliefs can make a heaven of hell and a hell of heaven, witness if you will the demise of the financial whizz kids, business leaders, world leaders and the ubiquitous rock/sports stars as they continue to ask upon arrival at the home of their dreams...is this all there is? It is, if they believe it to be so.

More on the unreasonable nature of a Big, Big Dreamer.

This core element, the *attitude of breakthrough unreasonableness* is central to the achievement of your big dream. How many dreamers of the night do you imagine think about what to do, but then become frightened, lose their nerve or believe they will not succeed under any circumstances, because there will always be something in the way, something preventing them from fulfilling their dreams? How many dreamers of the night do you imagine acknowledge that they don't know that they don't know what to do and so just do anything in order to appear productive? How many dreamers of the night do you think are adept at adapting themselves to fit the description of the reasonable man as George Bernard Shaw wrote...'The reasonable man adapts himself to the world, the unreasonable one persists in trying to adapt the world to himself, therefore all progress depends on the unreasonable man'.

Being unreasonable in thought, imagination and actions every day takes some doing, but it becomes the spine, the invisible thread that forms the join between the desire and achievement of our greatest dreams. And so right here and right now, imagine, if you will, the feelings of transforming into (and change can happen in a moment, you'd agree with me wouldn't you) an unreasonable big, big dreamer unwilling to take no for a final answer because what if as Anais Nin says 'We don't see things as they are, we see things as we are'...and you began to remodel and restructure around this re-awakening an overwhelming belief in yourself as an achiever, a person of conviction, an action taking momentum creating big, big Dreamer of the day, how does that sound and feel to you, right now. Look at the facts, you have read this far, you have come so far in your mind, and you are a physical miracle, a quite brilliant individual who no longer needs fear their own gifts and powers, which really means you are now looking into an inner world so incredibly vibrant and alive, the only question you ask for the moment is how the heck did it take me so long to reach this place.

"Everything you can imagine is real"

Pablo Picasso
The Dream (1932)

And this realisation that you are not so much 'the special one', or that there is anything necessarily vaguely mystical or magical about you, that indeed you are an ordinary person that happens to be living an extraordinarily big, big dream is what sets you apart. You see the miracle within and act upon it, most do not, because almost everyone has the potential, the opportunity to live a life of miracles and to dream big, big dreams that only a child can dream, yet few dare use it, even fewer still desire and hunger to live a life to the full.

And it is these very same limiting models or maps of the world which reasonable people have which are now defining how and what they are achieving in life. blissfully unaware that what they see, hear and experience every day has been filtered, deleted, distorted and generalised in order to give them what they want and confirm what they believe they are worth.

And that's precisely how dreamers of the night continue to limit their choices. It is not the world that is limited in choice, it is the ordinary, reasonable dreamer who is limited because they block off any of the possibilities and opportunities open to them, since they are not available in their map or model of the world. After all no map can show the rise and the fall of a city nor the slopes and holes in the ground, nor either the smells and sounds therefore unreasonable dreamers know that the map, the mind, is a good guide to experience but it is not in actual fact, the territory they live in.

Reasonable dreamers come to bemoan their bad luck, their timing, and the effects of the credit crunch, the lack of perceived resources, a recession and rising inflation upon their standard of living. They lower their expectations and filter out, generalise and distort their experiences to make them consistent with what they have been told to expect.

And thus ordinary dreamers create very few rich experiences to challenge these generalisations, their positive expectations are confirmed, and the cycle continues. In this way ordinary dreamers maintain their impoverished and unfulfilled models of the world.

Paradoxically, big, big dreamers enrich their model of the world by reversing this strategy, thus creating expectations of what they want to happen in their world framing events in ways which help them remain on track to succeed. Thus they create their own success fuelled self-fulfilling-prophesy.

This is the flip side of the impoverished world-view of ordinary dreamers, and it follows that the Fresherneur deletes, distorts and generalises events and experiences into opportunities and high expectations, engaging and embracing outcomes and feedback in order to add value to whatever venture they are engaged in.

Think Opposites...Think Why not?

Paul Arden, 'the advertising and marketing genius', formerly creative director of Saatchi & Saatchi says in his wonderful book *whatever you think, think the opposite*, 'If you hear yourself saying 'you shouldn't do that, then you must go out and do it'. Big, big Dreamers are rare because they do just that, and do it regularly which is most uncommon. Reason is one of our most wonderful gifts without which we would be victims to mysticism, myth, martyrs and mayhem, yet to discover the essence of life, as Aristotle might say 'the what it is' ie life's composition you must come from the opposite direction and not always bow down to the voice of reason and rationality that warns of rejection, failure and disappointment. You are not to be fearful of developing opposite thinking; you are called to embrace the uncertainty of it all because winners and big dreamers go out and fail, get up and learn, go fail again, take responsibility and become remarkable in the process. They go out and astonish people with their actions, their values, their works and the extra one percent. They under-commit and over-deliver, under promise and continually astonish people with what they do. They know there is so little competition to thinking opposite to everyone else. Thus you must become someone who is prepared to listen to others and yourself and then go the opposite direction if it feels right, if it's instinctive. You are then becoming the kind of person who is going to achieve your own big dreams, by thinking opposites and going on instinct, belief, trust and audacity.

Ask with Audacity and with Skill...

Here is a tip from a very unreasonable friend of mine who said 'Russ if there is anything I can pass onto you that others might use profitably it is this - ask, ask and ask again and even more so, ask with intelligence. Ask in a way and within a time frame that allows people to help, lets the other person know you are respectful, someone worth believing in and worth helping'.

Successful big, big dream achievers like to be given the opportunity to give back, to help someone else to succeed. The unreasonable thing to do is to ask and expect a positive answer. So go ahead and ask for that job, ask for help, ask for the opportunity and ask for responsibility. Ask for the pay rise you feel you deserve and then prove that you deserve it, by making yourself invaluable. Ask for advice from someone more skilled than you. Ask for advice from someone in a different sector to you and you will definitely be surprised at the results of asking intelligently for what you want, as the truth is that most successful people want to help someone they perceive as helping themselves.

Be unreasonable, ask for help from the leading players in your field, or even another field altogether. Ask in person, ask via email, ask in the third person, but ask the question. Can you help me achieve my big dream; this is what I've done so far! One of my earliest memories of asking, and asking with intelligence for help with one of my biggest dreams, was a time I asked and asked with persistence, intelligence and determination, until the question itself became unstoppable and demanded an answer. See...what if you discovered your hero, your role model, mentor and confidante to Presidents, Fortune 500 leaders, world class athletes and people of so many different nationalities across the globe was coming to town. And this person inspires thousands upon thousands to attend his seminars, paying at least £500.00 for a seat, yet what would you do if you were flat out broke, what could you do?

If you knew he was coming to town, but you were flat broke yet you totally knew you must attend his seminar (the backdrop being that most of my peers were bragging about going and what they were going to do when they got there, etc.) So what would you be thinking, what would be going through your mind if this incredible icon was coming to your country for the very first time with a media, political and celebrity frenzy, all vying to get tickets to the hottest show in town? His name wasTony Robbins, the world's leading Peak Performance Coach. I knew I had to be there, had to see him, talk with him. Failure was not an option. Some people say that luck occurs when preparation meets opportunity and it was right there and then that I made a decision to act unreasonably. First I had to begin to imagine, was it possible? Possible to connect, possible to engage disparate images, sounds and feelings in my mind and body in ways I never had before. I knew I had read a wide selection of Tony Robbins articles and books, including a chapter within a bestseller of his (Unlimited Power) called 'The Power of Precision,' which was about asking yourself and others a better quality of question in order to get better quality answers. In his book Robbins had described with precision how to ask questions of the person you wanted something from, and how to ask with intelligence, namely by finding out what that person most values and aligning yourself with those values. Remember how I said earlier that heroes leave tracks, they tell you things that can save you years if you use them? Well Robbins went on to explain his own strategy for giving an affirmative response to a request, and in the process I was able to define (remarkably) Robbin's values and criteria for giving.

I knew also from Robbins' best-selling books and articles that he once lived in Marina Del Mar, California. So I made haste to write to Tony, but this was going to be no ordinary letter. This letter was unreasonable, a letter I had never imagined before, both original and framed in a specific way that matched Robbins' stated strategy for **saying 'yes'**. A reasonable reality of course, or at least one reality (remember what I said about how we delete distort and generalise information to prove our expectations and beliefs true) was to say that I had no experience of success, ever, in getting a very successful person to say yes to me.

And not only would Robbins be saying yes to me, but yes to effectively letting me into his seminar, which was over-subscribed, yes to me not paying the £500.00 for the privilege, and yes to so many things that I even now cannot imagine.

Indeed if this was so outside my experience why would I try? What would an ordinary dreamer have done in the circumstances? (Answers on a postcard, please ☺) I didn't, of course, have any idea that Robbins would even see the letter, let alone reply. Even if he did see it, would he read it, would one of his employees read it first and throw into file13? Even if he did see the letter would he be true to his word? All of these and many more questions poured through my mind, yet I knew that if life all comes down to a few unreasonable moments (and who is to say it doesn't) then this was certainly one of those moments.

So I decided on one simple thing. To believe! To believe he would get it, to believe he would fulfil my biggest of dreams at the time. And so the letter was sent with faith. (Truth without proof (sic)). The result! A day passed, then a week and then two weeks and nothing, three weeks and still zilch nada. So, in the spirit of unreasonableness, another letter was sent to Robbins and another two weeks passed with no return, and time was passing quickly.

My beliefs were being firmly put to the test. If he didn't come through for me soon, what do I do next? If I was to go to Tony Robbins' three day seminar I had to, I must get a result soon. So another six letters went off to Del Mar and still nothing. So I sent another twelve letters. I was either going to be very successful or arrested for stalking. Realising there was nothing more I could do I chose to rest and let it go; I had done all I could.

Some seven days later, roughly 42 days since the original letter was sent, at approximately 11.30am the telephone rang and it was Robbins personal assistant. She had a beautifully rich Californian edge to her voice as she proceeded to tell me that Tony had received my letters and was totally blown away by the content. He wanted me not only to have a ticket for his seminar, but he personally would be very pleased if I would go there as one of his special team members, helping in the preparation and organisation of the seminar. When I lifted myself up off the floor, still not fully perceiving what had just occurred, I of course accepted Robbins' magnificent offer with gratitude and just a little blown out, blown away joy.

You can imagine the kind of day I had telling my peers the news! Robbins had stayed true to his word. This would stay with me for the rest of my life as I now knew that it is possible to make the impossible happen. I asked the question and asked intelligently. I went out to Birmingham to the Robbins seminar and had three of the most awesome, life changing days ever, working behind the scenes, making sure I gave the best I had, whilst making sure I got the very best Robbins had to offer, giving everything I had toward his success for the seminar.

This story is not dissimilar to the one Robbins tells when as a young boy he managed to get an interview with the famous sports reporter Howard Cassell. How did he do this as a young boy? He took a chance and asked. Robbins never forgot the experience either.

Walking alongside Tony Robbins at 0300 on a cold and misty Birmingham morning, I watched in awe, cuckooned within an aura of heartfelt warmth, gratitude and increasing fascination... and just a little intensity ☺ as he helped to build the thirty foot long fires that just a little later nearly 2000 people would walk across helped by me!! I had been chosen to motivate the people in the lines to assist them in making the leap, and then doubling up with a hose pipe at the end of the burning hot coals, making sure everyone had nice cool feet at the end. There is no doubt that I was living the big dream and I had made it come true using one of the tenets of the DNA code of becoming a successful big dreamer. I asked and asked intelligently and followed through with unreasonable no quit actions, and a belief that I would receive a positive answer.

And so to recap… unlocking the code.

Find your purpose, your passion, the reason behind the dream. Begin with the end in mind. Begin with the dream fulfilled, seeing, hearing and experiencing it the way you want it and then bringing the good feelings forward to the present, now.

- Believe with all your heart in your big, big dream
- See it, experience it as complete and always learning
- Find someone who's already done it
- Be unreasonable in thought and action every day
- Create momentum through action
- Decide never ever to give in
- Remember, people want you to succeed

Your decision never ever to give in, to find a way, come what may, can be the defining characteristic in making your big dream unstoppable. There is no doubt that people recognise someone who has made a personal decision that there is nothing on this earth that will prevent them from succeeding. It is most certainly a different level of thought and action that carries you toward your dream. You become unstoppable because you believe you are. You become creative because you believe you are and you'll take any and all actions necessary and legitimate in order to succeed and achieve.

NO TURNING BACK...

A person who burns their bridges in order to prevent any thought of turning back is a person both literally and metaphorically destined to achieve everything they could ever want because there becomes nothing that cannot be turned into learning and positive feedback, given in order that you may succeed. When you burn your bridges there is no way back to what you were before, no way back to your old programming and processing, no way back to familiar territory, situations, people and crutches. If you were ever to look back in fear or trepidation, hold on because where you are is an indication of where you are going. Remember fear isn't to be destroyed it is to be harnessed and used to help you so don't look to the past, instead look to who you are and who you are becoming because that is where you will find what you need everytime.

There is always something to learn, results to turn around and actions to change. Things happen for a reason, because that's the natural order of the universe and they occur for you to learn something, to move you forward to another level of thought, plan and action. Now, I don't know if it will take you a month or two, maybe as long as three months, before you notice the changes in your behaviour, capabilities and beliefs and what you can achieve, but what I do know is that when you truly commit there can never be a return to what was.

So as you arm yourself with an unbreakable never ever give in, no turning back attitude to becoming all you can be, you will have set in motion a cause and effect scenario where upon whatever happens, the meaning of that event will be yours to define positively, rather than some burnt out old programming that probably has less and less value in your life. Quite simply you are adding one of the most important and valuable pieces of armoury to your tool box that will hugely determine how you fare in life along the way to becoming successful with momentum.

Find your passion
and you will find your purpose...

Find your passion and your purpose will reveal itself. There is something bigger than you and your dream, and it is to be found in your purpose. It has been said that the way to achieve your big dreams is to help others to achieve their own big dreams. Maybe your purpose is to entertain, to make people happy through your skills, your creativity and originality, to delight and develop good positive feelings for those around you. What if your purpose is to make sense of history by passing on what you learn through your adventurous times to other big dreamers, dreamers who have little real chance of becoming all they can be, because something had been perceived as missing?

Maybe that something is to learn from the significance of the negative events in life, or maybe even your life, and how you turned things around, not that they are to feel poor or bad or not good enough in the moment. But rather, how are they going to use events to move forward?

So ask yourself the question 'what's the bigger picture here, what am I missing, not yet seeing but could be very significant?

Talk yourself up...
(If you don't no-one else will)

Learn to quieten the negative self-talk that puts you and your dream down. Learn to turn things around so you're looking for and experiencing the most positive and powerful meanings and contexts you can create for yourself. Learn what I call talk it up time, which is something akin to transformational self-hypnosis. Every day go inside and turn up the volume of your- self appreciation and inspiration. Listen, watch and work the internal musicians and producers within your mind as you play your favourite tracks from your internal and external library and remember we're all different, maybe it's the sounds of Rachmaninov or Beethoven or perhaps it's the imagery of Dre, Jay Z, The Beatles or Oasis. It could be the energy and dynamism of Beyonce or Lady Ga Ga or could it be striking imagery of the Roman Coliseum, the Taj Mahal or a famous scene from a movie or something from your personal history. Now it's time to amaze yourself as you turn up the volume and size of the image...and then turn it up some more, and watch and listen as you experience incredible inspiration while you begin to appreciate yourself and those around you who love you and want to help you achieve your big dream. Begin to learn and use the power and richness of your language patterns to motivate and inspire you toward your great dream. As an example, can you imagine having a mind-blowingly awesome day, before the day starts? So how did you do that, who did you meet, what did they say, what did you learn today that made it better than yesterday?

On Feeling Awesome...

Someone said you can't afford the luxury of a negative thought because its effects have a ripple effect on the rest of your mind and body. If you're feeling bad about something you've experienced, said, heard or seen, then that feeling will remain with you until you change what you are seeing, thinking and experiencing, and your behaviour will reflect those emotions. So instead of an event occurring, for example, someone putting you down, and you becoming locked in the kind of perpetual negative self-talk, which affects how you feel; and so influences what you will ever attempt to do.

I am suggesting you turn the event around 360 degrees in your head by asking yourself a new question...Ask yourself 'what else could this mean'? It could mean 'this person can't handle my energy, my exuberance, or my desire for success' or it could mean 'there is an opportunity to learn here, about me and my ability to handle criticism and about the other person, what has to be going on in his or her life to make them put me down in such a way'? Let's take another example of seeming negative self talk... 'I need x amount of money to make y happen, which means I'll never make y happen', this becomes an opportunity to say to yourself that what may have been the case in the past is different now, that you trust in yourself and your ability to create and manifest that which you need, and that if you keep on working, keep on keeping your eye on the prize what you need will appear. These two examples reflect how two seeming negative events, which could have previously have had negative self-talk and behavioural implications become an opportunity to 'talk yourself up', positively. By turning potentially negative situations into positive opportunities to understand, reflect and move forward, you develop the real and valuable skills of emotional intelligence, to pause and talk things through with yourself before moving on toward the prize. What an opportunity for you to tell yourself how proud you are for standing up to other people's inability to empathise with your passion or appreciate your difference. What has happened is that by using your self talk positively and intelligently you have reframed or redefined the meaning of a given situation to mean something that strengthens you, keeps you focused and moves you forward with action and momentum. Crucial!

Ultimately, you can begin to feel better about yourself by planting the seeds and patterns of feeling good in any situation via your internal language, *your talk it up time*. So now, when and where can we put this into practice by installing the programme of *talk it up time* in your wiring so that when you need it, it becomes automatic? What if you were to imagine just before falling asleep, sometimes called the alpha state an emotional and physiological state of awareness that is relaxed, but aware, talking to your unconscious, (the part of you that remembers and knows everything about you and does everything for you just out of conscious awareness, such as holding blood pressure at a steady rate, and maintaining blood flow around the heart,)…to bring together into consciousness, first thing in the morning, the finest of your acheivements, past present or imaginary that you have ever known, and to spread that feeling of awesome, immense success and appreciation around you throughout the night and through the following day and to be especially present during any testing or challenging times, allowing you to call on all your incredible resources and strengths at will, this is called pro-actively *talking yourself up* , or future pacing, looking ahead to an event and procuring your greatest of strengths and resources to secure a better outcome, and using this influencer imaginatively and positively to look, sound and feel awesome.

For all challenges you face during the waking day, approach them with courage and with what Susan Jeffers describes in her great book '*Feel the fear and do it anyway*', as a sense of knowing that *"whatever happens you'll handle it"*. You know one can never escape fear, but you can accept it, face it down and just do the thing, no matter what, repeating to yourself with conviction,' Whatever happens I'll handle it, so I'm going forward anyway', that way you *develop courage which Churchill said is the quality that allows all others.*

Challenge fear –
by asking quality questions
and expecting positive answers...

In any tough situation ask yourself...

1. What am I doing internally that's helping to maintain this challenge in my life and how can I change what I'm doing to get a better result.
2. What if it's not the reality, it's just how I'm experiencing it now
3. What's great about this and how can I turn this around now?
4. Who do I know that's faced similar challenges and has turned it around?
5. What needs to happen to turn this around? How will I know when I have?
6. What do I want from this situation? What do I want to keep from this event that might be useful to me in the future?

7. What would (for example) Richard Branson, or Oprah Winfrey or Kelly Holmes do differently? What would they say to me right now? What advice would they give me?

8. Is there anyone I can talk to about what is happening?

9. When, where and how have I faced and come through this before?

10. If I were advising my best friend in this situation what would I suggest?

11. What are the implications for me, and my wider system if I continue with this line of thought?

Plan to Succeed...

Focus and plan your dream. Start at the end, having achieved your goal and work your way back asking yourself the question 'what has to happen now in order for me to have achieved this last step?' For example if your big, big dream is to own the car of your dreams, what must happen before the showroom salesman hands you the keys to that brand new motor? You have to be in the showroom to pick the car up, but what had to happen before you arrived in the showroom to pick the car up? Answer? The financials, and what will have to have happened for them to be completed and agreed? Now ask yourself the question what had to happen directly before the financials were agreed and completed? Maybe you agreed on the choice of car

Can you see how you just simply work your way back to the beginning of the dream, and then you will have a completed plan for your big dream. Now you can experience the great feelings of ownership and take them back with you, and yes you will slip and stumble, (because the map is not the territory) but that's a must, as *failure is a pre-requisite* for any success. Work your plan and big dream every day in order to create unstoppable momentum. All successful big dreamers have created a plan to achieve, either consciously or unconsciously, yet remember it has and never will be enough to dream and plan without action. Every day have courage. Take small, unreasonable actions, build momentum and momentum will build confidence, which in turn can take you incredibly fast forward toward your dreams.

Without your vision, your action, your plan, your feedback from failure and success, and without momentum, you can miss your time, miss your opportunity. There are many other ways to create a workable plan to enable you to move toward your big dream. The most prolific one and used most often by Big Dreamers, achievers of their greatest dreams, is to find someone who has *achieved* a similar dream to you; just an approximation and then you re-model it. Modelling, working someone else's plan helps you find the key steps that the individual took to succeed and to follow them, often saving you invaluable time and energy.

Find the beliefs that took them there, the physical actions that advanced them and drove them forward toward their big dream. There is someone somewhere who has succeeded in what you want to do, it could be in the same field or a totally different one, it doesn't matter. What does matter is that you look, ask, take action and follow the plan all the way through. With the almost omniscient presence of the internet, plus books, CDs and DVDs it is almost impossible not to succeed. Not to get started. We are at a point where many believe we may never return, one filled with an abundance of riches and opportunities, where you can start a business in a garage and within five years become a billionaire, or create something so special it will outlive you, creating a legacy that one person or one billion people will benefit from. Many of the achievers of our time have written books detailing their strategies often with step-by-step plans of how they have succeeded. So grab the plans and work them in order to succeed and waste no time in this endeavour.

Time: The Most Valuable Commodity

A millionaire friend of mine told me the one thing you can't hold on to is time because the moment right now can never be recaptured and so every second counts and will never ever be repeated. Consequently every experienced and successful big dreamer has a tremendous appreciation of time and timing. Big Dreamers, winners, dream achievers like you eventually develop a wonderful appreciation of time and timing.

    Listen; imagine being told you had just 56 days to live. How would that change how you think and do and your appreciation of time? What would you do now that you fundamentally believed you couldn't do? What wouldn't you do right now, how would you do it and with whom? Where would you go and how would you see, hear and experience people and events differently. How much more would you laugh, cry, enjoy, give, support...how much more would you enjoy being in the moment. How would time or a lack of it change your perceptions about yourself, other people and what was possible here and now? Yet look back now, to all intents and purposes you haven't got just 56 days to live and you can see, can you not, just how much more became almost instantaneously open to you purely because you shifted your perceptions about time and its meaning to you.

So, given the rest of your natural life back now what will you do in this moment? Did that change your strategy, your actions and your view of results and reality?

Did that change your style of doing things; have you made a decision to to succeed? **You bet you have, haven't you.**

How quickly did you find uncommon success? Who did you talk to and how far did you go in order to make that talk? Who did you no longer take 'no' from? Did you Remember Goethe's saying 'if one moves boldly toward one's dreams then one will meet with uncommon success in a very short time'. What if every day, having made the decision to value your time in ways that you never had before, you decided to squeeze every last drop of juice out of every moment? What kind of real differences would that make to you, now you come to think about it?

Caught up in the supreme adventure that is your life you create a universe where, like Einstein, you create an environment where you feel you are travelling on a beam of light, instead of having limitations and borders placed around you by time, people, events and past decisions there is an adaptation of time in the Einsteinian sense of the world as you become time itself with no right or wrong, up or down, just a flow state that puts you in a frame where you are neither comfortable or challenged beyond your capabilities, you are in the zone, an unstoppable and irresistible force. The question for you is no longer if, but when, no longer why, but how specifically. You are in an area of timelessness as every achievement has a cause and effect, every action you take creates a result, something you can learn from, take heart from and move further toward your big, big dream.

If you have ever thought that your time is up or over or through and you can do no more, then think again, because that is precisely the route that the culture sets out for us, that there is a time limit to achieving our big dreams. Our culture couldn't be more wrong. If you have the desire, the sensory awareness, the emotional intelligence, the passion, motivation, vision and persistence to take consistent daily actions that create momentum in your life then you will succeed. If there is a physical timeline on your goal, whereby you must be physically capable of succeeding in a certain timeframe, then yes you must appreciate that fact, but be open to changing the doors of your perception, because there are many ways to reach your big dream as people appear in order to help you as long as you have a growing appreciation of time and of people's time. The more you believe in yourself and your timing the more the right people appear. Armed with the right application to learn, to fail, to change, to get better and stronger, physically and mentally, emotionally...you will be giving yourself the chance to succeed. This is what is meant by understanding and valuing your own and other people's time. You see it's never been about the race, more like a marathon, a journey of self-discovery over time, a powerful and influential discovery about yourself that leads you away from the familiar existential cry of 'is this all there is', to a wonderful sense of Joie *de vivre,* the pure joy of living, loving and discovering in the moment.

You see when we unnecessarily bind ourselves within unreasonable and false time constraints we limit our chances and opportunities to succeed and ultimately fail, and so right now, if you are feeling bounded by time, try this exercise. Just stretch out your arms and, in your imagination, just push the boundaries back as far as they will go and open up the vista(s) in front of you (as I have just paused to do), and breathe, giving yourself freedom to slow down because if time constraints are constructed by us then they can be deconstructed too, can't they.

Understanding time, how it flows and how we use it, are valuable lessons in the quest for success and achievement and are the keys to the flow state we desire in our attempts to achieve our big dreams. Donald Trump, admittedly not everyone's cup of tea, has stated frequently that if you're going to dream then you might as well dream big dreams, if you're going to think, then think big. I'm in complete agreement with 'The Donald' on this one, as the bigger the dream the bigger the motivation to achieve and succeed. The bigger the dream the bigger the resources we need to call upon. I am convinced that we cannot live without a big dream, without hope. They (big dreams, big hopes) pull out the best of us through our imagination, our ability to see clearly ahead of us…to see, hear and feel our future Big Dreams achieved before any real physical acknowledgement of achievement. Big dreams draw big people toward us, people who want to help, give and inspire, who want to mentor and coach us. Some require payment and some don't – you will know what is right for you intuitively. Big Dreamers everywhere, from Da Vinci to Isaac Newton, have given us some of our finest moments as human beings and continue to inspire genius to this day. Who inspires you and who do you inspire, who do you motivate and give to every day? Every successful person I have ever met, or read about, has started with a big idea and believed in it, believed in themselves and their purpose. The difference between successful Big Dreamers and a reasonable dreamer is belief, a sense of purpose, perseverance and action. Without belief there is no foundation for when things go wrong, no platform to sustain you when you inevitably fall. With self-belief, dedication and actions designed to move you toward your goal you will keep coming back and back and back no matter what happens along the way, taking more and more focused action to turn the simple dream into an unstoppable big dream for good.

Ultimately, I know you have big dreams, like millions across the globe. But the difference is you can call on resources, internal and external, that have propelled you toward becoming irresistible and unstoppable. This is one of the key ingredients of the DNA of a rich and great dream, which is to….Believe in big and to garner every possible resource that will come your way. Your big dreams are your motivation and drive. The big beliefs and small every day action steps are the fuel boosters you will need to reach your destination.

Run With Your Big, Big Dreams as if your Life depended on it...

Some people who write about achieving goals and dreams will often tell you that you must seek balance and equilibrium in your life. That you must have rest and give equally to the important values in your life... that you must give time in equal measure to physical and mental health, to economic and financial well-being and to social and relational matters important to you.

Well my answer to those people, based on my experience, is that in an ideal world you would do all of those things and more, you would apportion time and quality time evenly, and it would be the right thing to do, no doubt about it. In reality, when you have big dreams and for those dreams to be realised, balance, like mastery and perfection, is to be aimed for but rarely attained, at least in any straight line configuration. I realise this statement is highly contentious in differing cultures because we know how important balance is for our sanity, and so for many people, stating this view will be a step too far. I understand this viewpoint entirely, because for many years I too sought the chi, the way of harmony. I cannot say whether seeking balance makes us more or less of a person, makes us more or less likely to achieve our dreams. In the end each of us must make our own personal choice with regard to balance and decide to run with it. The ball is in our own court. For me the way of the big dream, the way of achieving your biggest and brightest of dreams is whichever way works for you and makes you happy. Every relationship suffers, and benefits, at some level from the selfish, for want of a better word, needs of the big dreamer. And so for me this is the choice, we can take up the baton and run for our lives, like our very existence depended on our success, or we try, and in the process pull ourselves apart, by attempting endless balancing acts in our lives. Balance is admirable, that is why as a culture, we seek it so deeply, miss it so badly. Yet our values will lead us in the right direction without creating schizoid personality structures, trying to please everybody, but ultimately pleasing no-one. So trust in yourself and run as if your life depended on the achievement of your greatest and biggest of dreams, and take those with you who want to be part of the ride, those that are prepared to support you come what may. It sometimes seems impossible to imagine that those kinds of relationships exist as far as the big dreamer goes. Yet forewarned is forearmed and, with the right and honest information given freely upfront, then it becomes possible for fulfilling relationships to take shape. These choices are not easy and there are many implications and consequences whichever way we choose – yet if we are to run with the ball and with our own game plan these are choices we cannot avoid.

And so here we are at the end of the beginning, concluding a first book that I hope breathes momentous new life into you Fresherneurs and soon-to-be achievers of your biggest dreams. The notion of dreaming big, big dreams within a child like frame, asking for a miracle and creating an unstoppable momentum are not new and I can't claim to have invented the genre yet what I hope is to have given fresh impetus, insight and experience to the millions of dreamers of the day, a term first coined as far as I can tell, by T. E. Lawrence of Arabia, in his book 'The Seven Pillars of Wisdom', in which you, both reader and Fresherneur, are inspired to dream and dream big, big Dreams, to become unreasonable in your quest, to take the reins and then run with your dreams to the ends of the earth…to help and to seek help wherever you go, to add more value to people's lives, and to live a life where you are burnt up rather than burnt out, and are able to look back upon your life and say 'I did it, I lived it and I loved it, I achieved the irresistible, the seemingly impossible. I showed I-am- possible (I'm possible) and made my greatest of big dreams happen…Remarkably.

Russ Meyers
Milan, Italy

Resources and Acknowledgements

Websites

www.anthonyrobbins.com

www.sethgodin.com

www.saladltd.co.uk

My incredibly positive and supportive family

Paul Arden

Anthony Robbins

Barack Obama

Bill Clinton

Dr John Grinder

Dr Martin Luther King

Dr Milton Erickson

Dr Richard Bandler

Donald Trump

Jamie Smart
Oprah Winfrey
Robert Dilts
Richard Branson
Susan Jeffers

Mihaly Csikszentmihalyi, author of "Flow:

My incredible sisters, Joyce, Barbara and Christine

[1]***Seven Pillars of Wisdom: Autobiographical book*** Recording the experiences of British soldier T. E. Lawrence ("Lawrence of Arabia"), while serving as a liaison officer with rebel forces during the Arab Revolt against the Ottoman Turks from 1916 to 1918.
(Wikipedia)

[2]**Fresherneur**, is an amalgam of the word Fresher, (first year student) and entrepreneur. I have found a fascinating definition of a student, being from the Latin second type conjugation verb 'studere', meaning to 'direct one's zeal at'. Hence a student is one who directs zeal at a subject. An Entrepreneur is (as if you needed me to tell you) is one who applies innovation within the context of business to satisfy unfulfilled market demand. (Source: Joseph Schumpeter 1934)

BECOME CHILD-LIKE
ASK WHY
ASK WHY NOT
IMAGINE
FLY

WHAT IF I COULD

WONDER

LAUGH

CREATE

LIVE

LISTEN

LEARN

BE CURIOUS

EXPERIMENT

BELIEVE

MOVE

Never give in - never, never, never, never, in nothing great or small, large or petty, never give in except to convictions of honour and good sense. Never yield to force; never yield to the apparently overwhelming might of the enemy.

Sir Winston Churchill
Speech, 1941, Harrow School

www.ingramcontent.com/pod-product-compliance
Ingram Content Group UK Ltd.
Pitfield, Milton Keynes, MK11 3LW, UK
UKHW041436180426
11947UKWH00007B/472